"You are not ashamed of your sin in committing adultery, because so many men commit it. Man's wickedness is now such that men are more ashamed of chastity than of lechery. Murderers, thieves, perjurers, false witnesses, plunderers and fraudsters are detested and hated by people generally, but whoever will sleep with his servant girl in brazen lechery is liked and admired for it, and people make light of the damage to his soul. And if any man has the nerve to say that he is chaste and faithful to his wife and this gets known, he is ashamed to mix with other men, whose behavior is not like his, for they will mock him and despise him and say he's not a real man; for man's wickedness is now of such proportions that no one is considered a man unless he is overcome by lechery, while one who overcomes lechery and stays chaste is considered unmanly."

— Augustine of Hippo, Sermons 1–19

Acknowledgements

Years went by as I carefully considered releasing this book. The names of those who have helped and supported me create an insurmountable list. However, I will attempt to thank those who were most relevant to this work.

The memories collected in Pervert go back to 2005. Along the way, I dropped out of school and worked minimum wage jobs, trying to find success elsewhere. But I soon re-enrolled in high school and graduated. No teachers supported my writing. Only friends whom I have cherished deeply till this day did. Cadden Hobbs, who is now prior military encouraged me to continue writing the stories that comprise this book. Craig Mack, who has become an unbelievable and excellent engineer, supported my writing from my first attempt. Kerry Cohen motivated me to aspire to become a writer and forced me to become a better mentor to others.

Thank you to the many men who have shared their stories with me and continue to be my friends. I hope that what I have shared with all of you over the years may help you find yourselves somebody decent, someone who will place you before themselves. I also hope that none of you make the same mistakes again.

Thanks to the uncountable women who have conversed with me while I was writing the book. You ladies were a big help and I am proud to call you my friends. At times men require a woman's input, and all of you assisted me.

Thanks to everyone attending Pima during my first semester of college there. I presented some of the stories of this book to complete strangers, and you all supported this and motivated me to keep writing.

Much love to my mother and father. Thank you for allowing me to grow by my own lights, so I would not have the attitude of the common young adult these days. If it weren't for you I would still be mad at the world for no reason, and expect everything to be handed to me like those fucktard college boys and girls whose way their mommies and daddies pay. I am extremely proud to have you as my parents, and will take care of you as you took care of me.

A special thank you to Alex and Jess Bianchi, who were there when I needed it most. Alex—there are no words to describe how thankful I am for all the small things you have done for me. Mark Bianchi, I will always be grateful to you for helping me with a job prior to my transition into the military, as well as for the hospitality of your home.

Thank you to Zach Hammer who motivated me to stay in physical and mental shape during the process of writing this book. And to Stephen Capps, who has been there for me through high school, college, and the military.

Thanks and gratitude to Meghan L. whom I knew only for a short period of time, who proved to me that strangers are often the best listeners.

Introduction

A rguments, lies, consistent paranoia fill my head. She tells me one thing that ends up becoming another falsity by word or deed. I lose my trust in her early on but still maintain the relationship. No matter how many times she lies or manipulates my heart, I am still there to be her rock, therapist, pillow to cry on. And her lies persist over and over again while I wonder why I'm still with her. Compromising in every way I can, I am still the one at fault and become the issue. No matter what I do, no matter what I say, nothing is ever good enough for her. My heart breaks. She either leaves or she cheats and yet I grovel for her to take me back, even though I was to blame for nothing. Wanting to be loved unconditionally and desiring someone to accept me for who I am. Wanting to be part of a commitment, to be forever happy with my mate.

I recall my days with my father, always strict with my sister and me. As soon as I moved out of his house, there were three things he had beaten into my head: be honest, stick to your commitments, and devote yourself to your goals. Pretty common stuff, right? My father was a retired officer with twenty-five years' experience. He was someone I had always looked up to, even though he and I never got along until I finally moved out of the house at twenty-one years of age. I never relied on him to talk to me when I was depressed, upset, or sad. He would consistently tell me to "act like a man" or "do something with my life." I respected his words and took them seriously. His honesty seemed brutal at times. During the time I lived under his roof I did look for emotional love in other places. I probably slept with close to thirty women. I kept a list in my head for a while, the idea of assigning myself a trophy for each partner. Then, I threw that idea away.

Women, I have found, are extremely excellent listeners or extremely excellent pretenders. Since I did not receive much emotional support at home, I would turn to women to feel loved, cared for, and seek commitment to fulfill my personal desire of finding someone who loved me for me.

Out of all the women I slept with during that time, I dated only three. One I married and divorced.

Most of the women liked to talk about themselves, spend time in the mirror ensuring they looked "beautiful," and rant about such things as their "cunt of a friend" who was a "total bitch," and their desires to "rip their tits off." Meanwhile thoughts would process through my head and conclude with a question every man would ask in this situation: "Then why are you two friends?" I do not ask them with sarcasm, just curiosity. I came to expect some bullshit response that contained nothing resembling logic.

I wouldn't expect anyone reading this to believe that I have always been sweet, mature, and a "nice guy." I am not innocent by any means.

This book is for the good ol' boys who have been through the torment, destruction, and perversion of attempting to find Ms. Perfect. It is for those gentlemen who believe in what it takes to keep a commitment and last through the best and worst of times only to see women pull away strips of their hearts, without a care in the world. I wrote this so I can show that men should not be painted as a specific picture of a woman's liking. If for example—as women often claim—men only desire sex, then wouldn't the ladies at least have to admit we are the most low-maintenance species to please? Let's not hold our breaths for that.

This book is also for the men who have done everything in attempting to make their woman happy and still question why they failed. I'm going to pop open another beer for you gentlemen and propose a toast to those who have felt alone after having done everything they possibly could. You have spent hours thinking about what you could have done differently. You bought flowers, planned dates, took her to her favorite place, and showered her with love.

…Yet, we're still the assholes.

Time builds a relationship. Through its rough patches and challenging hardships, nobody can expect to start a relationship and assume perfection from the first day to the last. This is how most of my relationships started: asking a girl to be my girlfriend and hoping for the best. I have seen women and believed I would smother them in gifts and love, treasure those private moments beneath the stars, and enjoy each other's company in a beautiful and romantic setting with candles and roses. *Watch me dazzle you with fucking sparkles and tell you I would bring you the moon.*

Fuck that stupid shit.

Most men hate doing these things and some men would be better off dating a person stronger than themselves. As for a guy who abhors pushing those efforts to make a woman happy, to display himself as someone who actually cares—regardless of my own thoughts of these over-decorated, over-romanticized evenings—we do it because we know it makes our women happy. There is a saying that goes "Happy wife, happy life." It holds true whether you're married or not. We enjoy spending time with our partner, but loathe the fact that overt, ostentatious displays are what many women genuinely like. I have never once in my life met a man who has said to me, *"I loved the candles and roses and adored the stars. It was so romantic."* You can argue I am insensitive. But I'm in the vast majority. As men, we would laugh at each other, or sling trash talk such as "Fag" or "Pussy-whipped." My personal favorites are questions like, "What's wrong with you?" or, "You date a guy?" The point is, men are stimulated differently than women. We like to see boobs, stare at your ass, and fantasize about what we would do with it. We do not require any number of courtships in order to cultivate this desire. However, this does not mean that we are completely insensitive and incapable of pleasing someone without the use of our penises. In spite of many excruciating experiences, I do not mind taking a girlfriend out on a date and showing her a good time. We do it because we feel good about ourselves and want to prove that we are worthy of pleasing our partner, and to show that we can be romantic. Like I said, if she is happy then I am happy. And I'm happy that I can **make** her happy. Men are generally the first ones to figure out what a compromise is. Women reading this may scoff, but it's true. We start out by doing some stupid shit date, spending our money, and expecting nothing from you. Hope is not the same as expectation, in case you were about to say what I know you were thinking. If we actually like you and aren't just trying to get into your pants, we listen to what you have to say and do everything we can to ensure you are having a good time.

Let's take a second and rewind so we're all clear here.

I ask a girl out on a date. I spend my money. I listen to her. I want to ensure she is having a good time. I expect nothing from her.

WHAT THE FUCK?

And usually, unless I tell her I invented MAC's makeup line or created the fucking iPhone she generally doesn't seem interested in my current job or everyday life. Instead we men get these bullshit interview questions that never appeal to us. The only reason we are most likely still at that dinner table is because she has a nice body, her life is in order, or she appears to be interested in the fact we could be the local garbage collector, and she is surprisingly okay with that.

There is no definition for how to "act like man" in any type of relationship. We have to make sacrifices, put our own desires aside, and grow with our partner. If there is anything I learned in my history of dating, it would be how to put myself aside and allow another to enter my life. Compromise and work together. Talk and listen. Become unselfish. Respect one another. Grow in love.

Prepare now for the parts of the book where I skip my life story and share my personal and sexual experiences of the women I have met in my life. Their names have been changed to protect their identities, I have also chaptered the stories of each individual woman in chronological order of my memory of them. It's been a fun ride, at times, and some might think the details are their own reward. But I came to understand a few important things that would have been worthwhile learning earlier, and they can't be explained without understanding what happened.

Jen

She was so perfect. Her coal dark hair, the way her blue eyes would collect a glimmer from the bright colors of her shirt. Her hair would darken in the winter and lightly brown in the summer. She illuminated with beauty that boys could only dream about. She was an ideal, a fantasy figure of someone I would want to be with. Sexually, first.

Summer was approaching and my middle school days were almost over. My stern father came through the garage that evening to speak with my mother and sister and me. I watched him place his keys on his old liquor bar and sit down at our round dinner table. My father turned to me and showed disappointment in his eyes. He cleared his throat and spoke to me as if I'd run up a cell phone bill.

"I'm not happy with your final grades."

I grew irritated with him quickly and reached for a glass of water at the table. "I passed all my classes," I told him.

He tapped his fork on the dinner plate and continued to avoid making eye contact with me. "You passed, with C's." He stopped tapping his fork and pointed it at me. "That's not good enough."

I began eating my food and swallowed. Turning to him I said, "Sorry," with no genuine care.

My father began to place food on his plate and sighed, "Me too. You're repeating the eighth grade."

I quickly collected my dinner plate and took it to my room upstairs to finish eating alone. No matter what I said to him, he would get his way. The school wouldn't have made me repeat. However, it was still my fathers decision.

There was nothing I could do at this point in my life, living under his roof. I chased girls through middle school and only wanted to have fun and act like a fourteen-year-old boy. As soon as the summer was over, I loathed the thought of repeating the eighth grade.

As school began again, I watched all the others who had moved up from the previous year. I had to deal with students asking me, "Did you fail?" or "Weren't you here last year?" I was upset and angry for the first few months, but eventually, I adapted to finding new friends and people who accepted me into their groups and cliques in middle school.

Then, just about every other day, I started finding love letters from girls, in my locker or taped under my desk. I found most of my days comforted by my first friends, Lauren and Lisa. Lauren was blonde, short, and very sweet to me from the first day of my repeated middle school days. Lisa was a brunette with blue eyes, skinny, and very cute. Lauren spent more time with me and would always walk with me in the hall and talk to me about her day, as well as inquiring how mine was going. She was the first one I had told about my home life with my father and the reasons for repeating the school year. She made me laugh and made me comfortable with where I was.

Half the school year went by. I changed my elective to a theatre class that Lauren recommended. I loved learning about the history of theatre and playing roles in the play. One evening after practice Lauren and I had walked out towards the parking lot to wait for her parents to pick her up. I could walk home after she left. We glanced at the front gate of the school and saw Lisa. My jaw opened and my eyes widened.

She was walking with a friend I didn't know, a girl named Jen.

I first looked at her ass, her hair, tone of skin, eyes. I wanted to hear her voice. I was already desiring to sleep with her, to know this girl, to romanticize and fantasize.

As the last two semesters flew by. I made every effort to find the routes she walked to class and where she was during lunch. I was over-my-head awed by this girl. During my last class of the day Lauren and I would walk past her and I would always smile at her and say "Hello." She would smile and giggle and continue walking. I wanted to pursue her until she was mine.

The summer came quickly. My father was happy that I had passed my classes with A's and B's. One night I received a call around two o'clock in the morning from a number I couldn't identify. I picked up and answered.

"Uh, hello?" I murmured.
"Hey," someone replied.

I heard giggling in the background.

"It's almost two in the morning," I said.
"Oh, it's Jen," she said, "I got your number from Lisa."

I let out a short laugh and rubbed my eyes. "I'm going to get some sleep. Call me later," I told her and hung up.

During the rest of the summer I didn't hear from her.

The preparation for high school started and I went about my normal days seeing everyone from my former class who were now a grade above me. I carefully observed those with whom I failed to advance and regretted having such a fuck of a dad.

But I saw Jen. We ended up having the same interior design class for our last period. We never tried to talk to each other during class. But we would wait for the bell to ring and would talk to each other after school. I would wait in the hall and be anxious to watch her walk out of the door behind me. She and I would walk outside and watch the school buses load and would talk to each other about homework and flirt. The only time we ever touched was when I would hug her goodbye, and then I would look forward to doing it all over again the next day.

This continued through half the school year. Eventually one night Jen texted me asking if we could talk at lunch, privately. I didn't know whether to feel excited or worried. During the school year I threw so many signs out that I liked her and wanted her. As soon as I met up with her that day she brought up what I had been too nervous to ask. "We should start dating," she told me.

I wanted to jump in excitement and scream at the top of my lungs.
"I think we should too," I responded.

We both smiled and walked away from each other. During the beginning of our relationship we didn't do many romantic things or even go see a damn movie, like normal teenagers.

Our relationship progressed and we began meeting up with each other after school. She and I would never talk romantically. What was a huge surprise to me was that we would sit by a local park and converse about school and the futures we hoped to find for ourselves. There was never use of words like "forever" and "always." We had each other, and it seemed to be enough. Jen however, was too irresistible. Her long dark hair, her blue eyes, and incredibly beautiful body would cause consistent erections when I was with her. Eventually during the time we spent together I would just look at her and think about sex. I had watched pornography multiple times during high school and fantasized about the sexual things that I wanted to do with her.

Every time I masturbated I would think of her and desire her body to be all over mine. Eventually this would grow into perversion that I couldn't fulfill.

Jen invited me over to her house one day. I didn't ask questions or make assumptions on my way walking to her house. When I arrived she grabbed my hand and pulled me inside. We walked through the house a bit, then suddenly she mounted me and began kissing me, placing her tongue in my mouth and rubbing her hand on my jeans where I was already erect. She had pink shorts on that barely covered her ass. Oh, how I wanted to have my hands all over it.

She grabbed one of my hands and placed it near her vagina. I slowly brushed two of my fingers against her clit, while kissing her on the neck and using my other hand to go up her shirt and press on her breast.

I took my time kissing her on the lips. She allowed me to suck on her neck lightly, feel her chest. I took my other hand and slowly pushed two fingers inside her. She breathed out deeply and stopped kissing me. Her eyes were closed while I felt around her. She didn't say anything and grabbed my wrist to go deeper. She then began to suck lightly on my neck. I took my other hand off her breast and onto her ass squeezing it lightly. I wanted her to touch my crotch so badly and I removed my belt. I continued to do what she was enjoying.

My right ear heard a loud sound. The garage door was opening and we both stopped immediately. Her father came in and acted as if there was nothing wrong or suspicious. I was in shock. Waiting for him to tell me to immediately leave or threaten to kill me. He acted as if nothing was out of place. Yet I believe he knew something was happening. Jen and I walked into the kitchen area as she poured herself a glass of water. Her dad came in and asked, "What are you two up to today?"

Jen and I looked at each other and shrugged our shoulders. It must have been obvious to him, but I didn't say a word. Jen and I later stayed out front of the house and kissed each other for minutes and hugged for hours. When the sun began to go down, I began the eight mile walk home.

After that, whenever we wanted to be intimate, we would set up times to meet at the park by her house. I would sneak out at night, around 10 or 11 o'clock, and bring a backpack full of blankets. I was always scared to walk out of the house and into the streets on my way to the park. I remember nights being chilly and windy and hearing noises in the neighborhoods. The trepidation of being seen by a police officer past curfew was top in my mind. Every time I saw headlights or heard a vehicle approaching, I would hide. It usually took around an hour to get there. Jen and I would lay on the playground structure and gaze at the stars and talk to each other. It was so romantic, I thought to myself. I believed they were the most beautiful moments I would ever share with a person. We would spend hours kissing and touching each other, intimately. We did this for a month. Every other day we would meet each other and do the same thing over and over again. The more I got to know of her, the more comfortable I grew. I wanted to further my dedication to her and eventually surrender my virginity. I felt doing this would mean so much to her, and bind us forever together as one.

Eventually I made friends with a couple of her closest counterparts. I started a close friendship with her friend Amy, who talked to me at school and would walk with me down the halls from time to time. We spoke one night about Jen. She let me know Jen had talked about giving up her virginity to me. I was surprised and excited. The only thing in my mind was what Jen might be thinking and whether it was something she really wanted to do. Most important to me was ensuring that Jen would be okay, and that I would not become something she would regret later in life if we ever broke apart. That was something I hoped would never occur. I envisioned us going through college together and somehow, some way making things work no matter how hard life got for us. I was committed to her from then on.

The next time I had to wait for my parents to go to sleep before sneaking out of the house. I had ensured that I packed blankets and condoms and showered, paying careful attention to cleaning my pubic area…all the proper steps I believed were appropriate. I wore freshly cleaned blue jeans and a black t-shirt with no logos. My hair was shampooed and conditioned with John Frieda's "Brilliant Brunette," which was something I loved using, and if anyone would have tried to judge me on my personal hygiene maintenance regime, I would discard them as soon as throwing away a sandwich wrapper. I knew, *Tonight's the night.* I was going to lose my virginity. She was too. We had the perfect set-up. As soon as I left the house I would reach the park in a little over an hour. I did not run to avoid sweating and growing fatigued. I thought through so many scenarios of how it would go. "Missionary?" I thought to myself. "That is appropriate," I answered. I was concerned more about how she would feel rather than myself. Everything needed to be perfect for her. She was giving herself to me and I knew it would need to go as she wanted it. I waited for her at the park by a swing set, and saw a dark figure approaching. It was her. We sat down on top of a park bench and talked about what we were going to do. She placed her hand on top of mine and looked me in the eyes.

"I want to do this," she said to me. My heart started to race. The blankets were already set on the ground near the bench. We began to kiss. I took my time and lifted up her shirt and removed it from her body. She put her arms around me and pulled me on top of her. Kissing, she reached her hands towards my pants and quickly removed my belt. I reached for a condom from my back pocket simultaneously and put it on. I stopped kissing her to look directly into her eyes.

"Sure you want to do this?" I asked.

She nodded her head. I hesitated a bit then slowly entered her. She pushed me back a little bit. "Ouch," she said, trying to keep her voice down.

"You alright?" I asked, worried.

She nodded her head. And we continued.

My first time was not something I had expected—staying in missionary position the entire time and unable to ejaculate. My focus was entirely on her, hoping that she was going to feel okay and not regret her decision later. The only thing that went through my head the entire time was concern for her feelings. I packed up my blankets in my backpack. She said she was in a little pain and I held her in my arms for a few hours afterwards. When I got home, I pulled out my blue blanket and found spots of blood on it. I showered after placing it into the washer.

Our relationship felt stronger at first, but arguments started to arise and we exchanged words over the stupidest little things. The only thing that I wanted to do was spend time with her and see her normally at school. There were days I felt ignored and as though I were a ghost to her. We would get past these small things and still meet up with each other after school and continue to sneak out at night. We had sex multiple times, but we never really engaged in any oral foreplay.

Jen invited me over her house on a weekend. I arrived and there was nobody home, so I knew we would probably still mess around with each other a bit. That day we were watching something on television, sitting on the couch. She began to kiss me and take off my belt. Quickly, Jen started to suck on my already-hard cock.

It felt so fucking awesome.

Before I could actually climax, I felt a sharp pain and asked her to stop. I took a look at my penis and saw a little blood, nothing too big, but I was worried I had a problem with my penis.

Jen's braces had cut me.

She looked at me and asked, "Are you okay?"
"Yeah, I'm fine...I think," I replied.

I went into the bathroom and applied toilet paper on the cut for a while, rinsed it with water, and spent most of the day with her watching T.V. while my penis ached.

Eventually Jen and I broke up. We were together for eight months and then completely stopped talking to each other. I made numerous attempts to be with her. However, Jen eventually gave me her opinion that I was a controlling asshole. I couldn't believe it. Every time we had argued I'd comply and let her win consistently, allowing her to have her way without trying to make a bigger argument out of anything she said. I challenged her, saying, "Wanting to make a plan with you and see you during school, lunch, or after class is not controlling." Jen had never been like this before, and it appeared to me she was looking for excuses to be out of the relationship. I chased her for about a year, attempting to talk to her from once a week to once every two weeks or so. She finally contacted me, and the final thing she said to me was, "I don't want to be friends with you or know you. Stop being a bitch about this." I never tried to speak with her after that.

My heart was broken. I didn't know what I'd done wrong to lose Jen. The time we spent together including the beginning of our friendship was a span of two years.

After the break-up, Jen and I would greet each other if we ever walked by one another, but she would act is if we were complete strangers and that we never shared anything emotionally intimate at all. I reflected on how Jen treated me after the relationship and decided that I was not going to put myself in that place again. She had made promises to always be with me, to care for me, and to love me. She mentioned that we would work out our problems and be friends. We had talked about our future through college and what we both wanted to do together as we grew older. All these things that I looked forward to disappeared. Jen was most of my life through the first two years of high school. Most of my friends never talked to me while we dated. The only two I had left from high school are still my friends to this day. I promised them at the time I would never blow them off again for another stupid girl.

My mother was a quiet person. I had tried to talk to her at home and found no emotional backboard. At first I wouldn't dare talk to my father about it. Eventually I tried to edit out the emotions, unsuccessfully. With tears running down my face, I told my dad that I had lost my virginity to Jen. He sighed and asked, "Were you safe?" That was the only thing he cared about. I told him, "I was." He went back to watching his T.V. I closed the door on the way out of his room.

Lisa

Eventually, Jen became someone entrenched in my past, but she still haunted me like lingering cigarette smoke in a tight room. Nights I no longer snuck out of the house and fell asleep early felt peculiar. I grew depressed and withdrew from high school. My father wouldn't speak with me most days which did not bother me at all since he would be at work. I became a night owl and would stay awake until dawn, blogging about useless video games or reading about the news and various politicians. Most nights I would tip-toe around the house and drink some of my dad's whiskey that he would leave out on his bar. I experienced my first drunk evenings all alone. My short time away from high school began to affect my social skills, and nights drinking alone soon became achingly lonely.

I enrolled in a charter school, taking classes that allowed me to sleep all day and start school at five o'clock in the evening, going to ten at night. The school allowed me to catch up on missed credits and even advance ahead. I thought about my old friends, but the idea of getting in touch with them came with a sense of hazard. I had spent the previous six months absent any socialization with old classmates. My computer and the darkness and my solitude had become my best friends. On the weekends I would scan social media and view what people were doing, watching updates from their sports, events, parties. This was enough, to stay in touch safely behind the computer screen. All I wanted to do was spend time alone and continue completing as many classes as I could.

Eventually one Friday, late at night, I received a message from Lisa, Jen's best friend. Or at least that's what I remembered. She asked me how I was doing and where I'd been. I opened up to Lisa and let her know everything was okay, and my plan for school was to catch up to my original classes. She and I would trade conversations repeatedly for months. I kept Lisa in my thoughts.

School came to its closing semester. I had caught up with classes to the point I was in the same grade level as my original class, the one I'd fallen behind when repeating the eighth grade. During the last two weeks of the semester a student I had seen around but never met before approached me.

"Hey, I have totally seen you before," he said.
I looked at his long blonde hair, glasses, and squinted my eyes.
"Did you attend my previous high school?" I asked.
"Yes! I remember because we had our lockers next to each other. I'm Justin," he said, holding his hand out for a shake.

We became close friends fast. It had been so long since I'd had someone to talk to about typically male things. Like me, he was a night owl, and we enjoyed each other's company with the same music, games, and appreciation for great books and philosophy. On some nights he would come over and just relax in my room, neither of us saying a word as we read or focused on schoolwork. Renewed companionship felt good.

My talks advanced with Lisa. One day she mentioned she would love to see me and that she missed walking with me through the halls at school. Being concerned about her relationship with Jen, I was cautious. She called that same night to see if I was interested in seeing her.

"We need to hang out. Like, right now," she said.
"Ok, do you even know where I live?" I asked.
"No, but you can come get me," she said, giggling.

Lisa gave me her address over the phone as I mapped directions on my computer. Justin was over, and I advised him I'd be back later, with her. I took my mother's silver 2001 Alero and drove to Lisa's.

Thoughts raced and questions swirled like a carousel in my head. "This has to do with Jen or something," I thought to myself. "Maybe she's just bored?" I mused. I reached Lisa's neighborhood and waited for her in a cul-de-sac with no street lights. I turned the car off and wondered, "Wait, is she sneaking out?" I saw a dark figure and the sound of a gate creaking in the distance. It was Lisa. I turned on my phone light and shined it through the window. She opened the passenger door and sat down.

"So eerie out there," she said, smiling at me.
"I know! Why do you live in such a dark neighborhood?" I asked.
"I don't know," she said, adding, "I don't sneak out that much."

Lisa and I began to drive back to my house. I was already wondering why she wanted to see me on this of all nights. It felt too random. Concerns over bringing Lisa in the house worried me as well. If my parents saw a girl in the house late at night they would cause a scene, and probably call up her parents.

"So what made you want to see me?" I asked, pulling into the driveway of my house.
"I've always wanted to see you," she told me. I lifted one of my eyebrows and stare at her. "This isn't about Jen is it?"
"Noo? She is being a total bitch to me. She and I haven't been getting along for a while now."

My eyes widened and images of Lisa and Jen walking around together at school filled my head. They were extremely close and there wasn't a reason I could believe why they wouldn't be friends.

"What happened?" I asked her.
"She throws attitudes at me, and I can't handle her being a cunt to me anymore."
"Anything specific happen?"
"No, it's a hit or miss with her. And I've just been absorbing all of her bullshit and negativity and I just don't want to deal with it."
"Well alright."

Lisa and I checked in with Justin who had passed out on the couch in front of the T.V. I turned the television off and went upstairs into my room with Lisa. I turned on my computer and T.V and sat on my bed with her. We talked about the previous years when we were in middle school. She mentioned the relationship that Jen and I had and asked, "Why did you two break up?"
"She was a bitch to me," I told her. "She just did a complete one-eighty."

Lisa and I talked about Jen for a while. She mentioned that Jen had been hanging out with new friends and appeared to care less about her old ones that she had had since middle school. I decided I didn't want to be too focused on the past with Jen and felt the urge to boycott any discussion that related to her. She needed to remain in the past, where she belonged.

"She is so manipulative," Lisa said. "It's so stupid."
Not feeling this left me an option to redirect the conversation, I obliged by asking, "What is?"

Lisa breathed in deep and blurted, "I had the BIGGEST crush on you in middle school and I think she was trying to be better than me."
I lifted an eyebrow, "So, she only dated me because you liked me?"
"Probably. Who knows? She IS a bitch."
"Well I didn't know that you liked me."
Lisa laughed. "That's because Jen would tell me how much she liked you. I was being her friend and backing off."
"I had no idea," I told her. "I thought we were pretty good friends."

Lisa lay on my bed for a brief second then propped herself up. She sighed and began patting her hands on her jeans and turned to me. "We could've worked, Daniel."
I nodded my head at her, "Yeah."

Lisa sighed and plopped back onto my bed, staring at the ceiling. A thought quickly hit me, "She and I could definitely do something right now." I turned to Lisa and stood up from the bed.
"I am going to get some water." I told her. "Do you want anything?"
"Water would be great actually."

I started to walk downstairs in my dark house and saw Justin passed out on the couch. I attempted to wake him up but decided not to after he rolled over. I went into the kitchen and poured two glasses of water and thought to myself, "I can either go along with this, or look back and wonder what could have happened." Walking back upstairs I entered my room and set the water down on my dresser. Lisa propped herself up and I handed her the glass.

"Thank you."

I walked back over to the door and closed it quietly. I then grabbed my glass and sipped on the cold, refreshing water while a movie played on my T.V. I turned to Lisa who had positioned her head to rest on the headboard of my bed.

"What the hell are we watching?" I asked.
"No idea, come here and watch with me."

I lay down next to Lisa and stared at the screen. She moved on her side with her butt close to my hip. It hit me that I hadn't wanted to have a relationship or date anyone since Jen; the only time I'd bothered looking at women had been purely due to basic sexual instincts. I'd been alone for what felt like years and had become immune to the loneliness. I realized the human connection I was pondering now was so unlike a basic friendship, like the solid nature of being able to hang out in a room without needing to say a word. The desire to enter another relationship that would require the level of care I felt so deeply for Jen simply hadn't entered my mind.

And realizing Lisa was lying next to me crowded out the philosophical thoughts. Attempting not to turn my head I stared down at Lisa's ass. "Fuck I want to take those off," I thought to myself. I slowly turned toward Lisa, and placed my arm and hand to act like a headrest. She didn't seem to mind I was an inch away from her. I tried to play it somewhat cute and softly placed my hand on her waist and moved toward her.

"So…why didn't you tell me that you liked me?" I asked.
Lisa repositioned herself towards me. "Well…I told you now."

I leaned in and made the smallest gesture I could to ensure she knew I wanted to kiss her. She leaned in and touched her lips with mine. The second I felt her skin I thought, "Well they are definitely not going to be best friends again." I expected Lisa to only kiss me. She threw one leg over me and propped herself on top. Hesitating, I kept one hand on the small of her back and the other feeling her ass as it rested atop my crotch. Lisa had one hand placed on my face and the other caressing my testicles through my pants. "FUCK," I thought to myself, "I've only had sex with one person." Variations on this realization caromed through my head as Lisa rolled to her side and pulled me on top of her. She put her hands up my shirt feeling around my sides and stomach. I took my shirt off and placed both of her legs around my body. "Fucking missionary dude. C'mon." I thought to myself. She started to press her mouth against mine. I slip my hands under her shirt and took it off. Simultaneously, she placed both her hands on my hips and pulled down my shorts as far as she could. They made it to my knees, so I moved back from her and took them all the way off to grab her pants from her sides and peel them from her. Hiding how much I loathed missionary position, I moved back on top of her. Lisa started to kiss my neck as I slowly pushed inside her.

"Slow…slow," she told me.
"Okay," I said, breathing out.

Lisa grabbed my hips, controlling how deep I went. She pulled me toward her. All intensity of sucking each other's faces off stopped. Lisa stared in my eyes as I pushed myself inside her over and over again.
"You can come inside me." She said, trying to keep her voice down.
I just about stopped, and wanted to throw her out of my bedroom window for saying that. But it felt so good….

"Do it," she told me.
Climaxing, my speed kept up only a short while longer and I came inside her.
"Fuck!" Lisa said, too loud.
"Shhh!!! Parents!"

Lisa lay in my bed for a moment then grabbed her water glass off the dresser.

"By the way, I'm on the birth control," she told me.
I made a short sigh and grabbed a towel from my computer chair.
"That's great," I replied. "Doesn't mean you won't get pregnant."

Lisa covered her mouth, hiding her smile as she laughed. She didn't appear to care that much, apparently more interested in the ecstasy of sex, and I couldn't really say I was any different. Lisa and I lay on the bed for another hour, and proceeded to have sex again and again and again....

I saw blue light through my window. I peered outside to see the rooftops of my neighborhood weeping for the sunlight's warmth to dry away the moisture of the night. Lisa and I checked the time—6:10—and hurried to get her home before her parents or mine noticed.

Dropping Lisa off, she kissed me on the cheek and started to head back through her back gate. I couldn't help but smile and think of what I had just done. "If Jen finds out she is going to be SO pissed off," I told myself.

During the drive back to my house I decided I wanted to keep this secret and wouldn't dare want to say it out loud. But that competed with the irresistible urge to at least tell one person. I decided it would be okay to at least let Justin know what had happened while he was crashed blissfully on the couch. I parked the car in the garage and woke him up, poking him a few times before he actually roused.

"Justin... dude," I said, looking to him as he started to rub his eyes. "What's going on?"

"I have got to tell you the craziest shit," I said, with a grin on my face.
Justin sat up and began scratching his head. "What is it?"
"I slept with Lisa."
"Okay, glad I was asleep for it then."
I paused for a second and rolled my eyes. "That was Jen's best friend.
One of her friends. They were close."

Justin leaned his head back onto the couch and smiled. "Oh shit dude.
She finds out then…"
I told him, "I know but she won't."

I sent a text message to Lisa expressing concern over the possibility of
Jen ever learning what happened. Lisa replied that she would never tell
and that it was our secret. It made me feel better knowing that Lisa was
on the same page but it was obvious to both of us that we still held
some care for Jen as a person and did not want to hurt her feelings. If
she had any left.

Justin went back to sleep and I was finally able to get some sleep
myself. We got up and around in the late afternoon. I took Justin home
and continued to do what I did best: be alone in my room and not speak
with anyone.

I spent hours sitting in front of the computer smiling every now and
then. Thoughts of how Jen was my first and Lisa, her best friend, was
my second. I didn't feel any emotional attachment with Lisa, but was
more proud of the fact that she desired me and wanted me. "I don't
want no fucking relationships," I told myself. But I wanted to feel loved
and wanted by other women.

🐇 <u>Sasha</u> 🐇

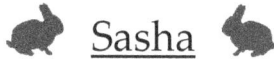

Summer's heat was quickly gripping the air toward the last day of classes. I thought about what I would do during the summer and felt I didn't have to be alone through the season. I went home one night so that I could message some old friends and catch up with them. I was able to reach an old acquaintance with whom I had skateboarded when we were very young.

Corbin was his name, a little big-boned but not fat, never really laughed but just had a calm way about him. He had dirty blonde hair and was always relaxed. Justin was still one of my friends during this time and we would still see each other at night. I would wake up around 4 to 5 in the late afternoons and skateboard with Corbin on those summer days. We would walk to the gas station or sit on the road and watch kids stroll by with their bikes and their siblings. Corbin and I established a close relationship.

I walked to his house one day to see him already skateboarding on his driveway. He was with an acquaintance I remembered from my old high school, Jake.

"Hey what's going on guys?" I asked as they laughed, looking into a cell phone.

Corbin covered his mouth as his face turned red. He flipped the cell phone towards me to show what was so hysterical.

"Look at this girl, dude," Corbin said. "She looks like a lawn gnome!"
I shook my head and turn to Jake. "Hey, man…haven't seen you in a while."
"You miss algebra class with good ol' Jake?" he asks.

I remembered him as a good guy, also relaxed and very calm. He was mulatto and very drama-free. He only enjoyed skateboarding and smoking weed. I didn't mind being around these guys.

"So what is so hysterical about this lawn gnome?" I asked, placing my skateboard on the concrete.

Corbin and Jake looked at each other and began laughing again. "She looks like a fucking lawn gnome dude," Corbin told me as Jake started rolling on the ground holding his stomach.
"There has to be more than that," I replied.

Corbin and Jake had gone to a party the previous weekend and met this "lawn gnome" between groups of mutual friends. I leered at the picture and thought to myself, "Yeah…I'd still fuck her though." Then I decided what the hell, and said it out loud.
"No!" Corbin says giggling. "It's a lawn gnome!"
I looked to Corbin and began laughing. "Alright, alright," I told him.
We continued our days skateboarding, which became custom to me. Soon after the school year started again, though, Justin dropped out of the charter school. I felt alone, with nobody to talk to at school, and reflected on the summer I had, skateboarding every day with Corbin and Jake. I decided to speak with my parents and enroll back into my old high school where they were, along with Jen and Lisa.

During the transition back to the school I decided to sign up for sports and try to become social again and meet new people. I decided I didn't want to be in front of my computer all the time doing nothing. Immediately on the first day back I linked up with old friends, Craig and Cadden, with whom I had made no effort to speak while I was gone.

"Daniel. Where the fuck have you been man?" Cadden asked me.
"Around, man. Doing my own thing."

Talking to Cadden felt alien to me. He had a group of friends that he would sit with at lunch and would only speak to me when I was changing classes around the halls, and even then I would only get a minor greeting.

I still searched for Craig, thinking he might not even be in school anymore. I decided to go to his house. When I arrived his mother was out front.

"Hey, is Craig around?" I asked.
"No. He is doing other things now." She replied, as she watched her two dogs sniff around the dirt.
"Okay, is there any way I could still get in touch with him?"
His mother sighed and looked at me with a blank face. "I think it would be better if you two went on your own paths."
I shook my head and drove back home.

I continued the school year and avoided crossing paths with Jen. I still kept in touch with Lisa but would never approach or talk to her at school during lunches. Corbin and I would hang around each other and create plans for the weekends. These would start with picking a place we could reach on our skateboards so we could commence with the drinking. Corbin and I were probably not the best duo to start a drinking habit. One night Corbin gave me a call to follow up on our plan to drink in a park that was part of our old middle school…the one I had attended for too long.

It was a baseball field hidden behind the desert. A safe place where all these kids would gather to drink a beer and act like idiots. I ran into my old classmates who had been ahead of me at one point and greeted them. They recognized my name but didn't show any concern as to where I had been. Some didn't seem to really care that I was there at all.

There were a few students that attended a different high school in another district. As I sat on a bench drinking Diet Coke and whiskey I noticed something familiar.

"Is that the lawn gnome?" I ask Corbin.

He approaches me with a joint in his hand and eyes red as blood. Corbin begins to chortle. "Yeah. That's the lawn gnome dude!" he takes a puff of his poorly-wrapped joint and walks over to Jake, snickering like a child. Jake and Corbin walk past me and look back.

"Daniel," Jake says, "C'mon."
I walk with them up to two girls, both very short, as Corbin and Jake laugh hysterically.
"LAWN GNOME!" Corbin says to this girl, hugging her.
She looks at Jake and hugs him as well.
My arms are kept crossed. I'm trying to figure out the relationship with Corbin and Jake. I look at her and smile.
"Why do they call you lawn gnome?" I ask.
She smiles and laughs good-naturedly. "Because I'm short. They're being idiots."
I smiled with her, "So is your name Lawn Gnome then?"

Laughing she places her hand out for a shake, "No, my name is Sasha."
Sasha is short, but nowhere close to the point of Walmart lawn gnome.
In fact she is about 5'4" with blonde hair that goes to her shoulders and
brown eyes. She is petite and light-skinned and sips on vodka and
cranberry juice. And I think she seems to have an attitude, but not a
bitchy one.

"Okay," I say, "No worries, I'll call you Sasha."
"I appreciate that."
I hear my name mentioned. I look over to see Corbin and Jake speaking
with another girl who seems familiar. I walk over with Sasha and see
the other short girl.
"Daniel?" she asks me.
"Mel," I say, looking at her and smiling.
"I thought that was you," she tells me.

I remember Mel as very sweet. She's the same height as Sasha. We have
known each other through mutual friends since middle school but have
never had a close relationship. Mel is a brunette, with brown eyes
and — I quickly discover — has grown to develop an extremely bitchy
side. She has the princess attitude all over her.

It's clear Corbin, Jake, Sasha and Mel have a good relationship with
each other and like smoking marijuana together. We stand in a circle
talking to one another as Mel, Corbin and Jake get high. As the night
passes I talk to Sasha about where she went to school and easy
questions about how she met Mel. It's a playful conversation and
having her as company is nice. We joke about the other three getting
high and later we find Corbin passed out in the desert, still high and
drunk off of his ass.

We close up the night carrying Corbin to his car. I take his keys and say goodbye to Mel and Sasha. Jake jumps in the passenger seat as I start Corbin's vehicle.

"Oh wait," I hear from outside the car. I roll down the window and see Mel approaching.
"What is it?" I ask.
"I'm doing a little get together at my place next weekend," she tells me. "If you guys want to come you can. It's going to be small, not too many people."
"Okay, sounds good," I reply.

Mel walks back to her vehicle where Sasha is waiting. I begin the drive home and do not think too much about anything regarding Sasha. I am more concerned over Corbin's drunk and high antics.
"He'll be alright," Jake tells me as he leans the seat back.
"Yeah, let's just get him somewhere to sleep," I tell him.

Monday arrived at school. I went on with my normal business and talked to my few friends. I found it easier to speak with girls than with the competitive guys running around trying to impress everyone. I had started friendships with more girls than boys, and whenever I would talk to a few guys they would make jokes that I was gay. Always being around girls and speaking with them, I found I didn't care much and felt more mature at this time in high school than most other boys. I only cared about the opinions of people I considered to be friends.

As soon as the weekend came around I linked up with Corbin and Jake. We were going to meet up with Sasha and Mel. A creepy twenty-six year old that Corbin knew purchased alcohol for us for a small fee, and we dropped him off after.

"Where the hell did you find that weirdo?" I look at Corbin, smiling.

"He just kind of walks around town. I've seen him hundreds of times."

We pull into the cul-de-sac and see two girls standing in front of a driveway. Jake has been talking to them over the phone while we searched for a place to park in the neighborhood. As soon as we park Jake hangs up the phone and taps me on the shoulder.

"You like the lawn gnome or something?"

Corbin and Jake look at each other and smile. Corbin reaches under his car seat and pulls out the bottle from the liquor store.

"No," I tell them. "I would fuck her, though."

Corbin opens his door. I look to Jake confused and walk up to him as he gets out of the car.

"Why do you ask that?" I say, as he looks back at me smiling and nods his head.

"Mel asked if you were coming. So I'm guessing she's asking for Sasha."

I smile and we walk toward the house with the two girls standing in the driveway. We greet Mel and Sasha with hugs.

"Why are you both just standing out here? It's fucking cold." I say, looking at them both.

They laugh.

"Okay," Mel says, "let's go inside now."

We follow Mel inside her house, I notice another girl on the couch who is wearing pink shorts and a white tank top. Her shorts barely cover her ass. It appears she is laying on the couch suggestively, with her ass facing the entrance of door we are coming through.

"Mel!" says the girl, sitting up from the couch.

"What do you want now?"

"One more please," she tells Mel.

Mel goes into the kitchen and gets a pipe for pot and hands it to her.

"Who is that?" I ask Mel.

"That's my sister, Amy. Fuckin' bitch."

I have no interest in meeting Mel's sister other than, of course, sexually. After Mel, hands her the pipe we walk into the backyard where a fire has already been lit. We sit down on metal chairs while Corbin and Jake and Mel pass a pipe around. I sit next to Sasha and talk to her. Corbin and Jake begin drinking from the bottle of cheap vodka, which I can smell as soon as they open it. We pass the bottle around as Jake and Corbin speak about obtaining more marijuana. This is getting into stuff I have never generally been around. Sasha and I watch the three bozos become drunk and high as the night goes on. She and I also become flirtatious, and a little touchy. She moves her chair closer towards me and places her hand on top of mine where I rest it on the chair. Mel looks at Sasha and smiles.

"You two need a room?" she says, laughing. Jake and Corbin begin to laugh as well.

"You drunk fucks," I say, smiling back at Corbin and Jake.

"Let's go get food," Mel says. "Sasha, you want anything?"

"Aren't I going with you?"

"Nope. You, Daniel, and Jake can stay."

Jake quickly takes another sip of the reeking vodka and hops up from his chair.

"Nope, I'm coming, fuck you guys." He says, zipping up his hoodie.

Sasha and I follow them out to the car.

"How long until you guys get back? Probably shouldn't be driving," I tell Corbin.

"Were just going down the street. It won't be long."

We watch them drive out of the neighborhood, concerned one of them will do something stupid, driving drunk and high. Sasha and I laugh and joke about them being idiots and began to walk back to the house. We stop at the front door as Sasha looks through the window.

"Let's go through the back gate," she says.
"Uhm, okay…Why?" I look at her, smiling.
"I don't want to deal with her sister talking to us when we walk in."
I follow Sasha around through the back gate and we walk to the fire that has been slowly burning out, its ashes sizzling in the air that has grown cold enough to begin stinging our lungs.
"There's a little bit more wood here," I say to Sasha, picking up a few pieces and placing them into the fire. We sit close to it. The wood is taking its time so I say, "Here, sit against me until it warms up."
"Okay."

I put my arm around her and say, "First time I saw you those two idiots were looking at your picture and giggling, saying 'garden gnome.'"
"They were probably stoned," she giggles.
"Yeah. I didn't know at first. I thought I was going to see something funny, and then they showed me your picture. I didn't get the joke."
"You don't think I look like an actual garden gnome then?"
"Only a little."

She elbows me and pretends to pout so I poke her in the ribs. She gasps and laughs, and says, "Stop!" I turn a little, shifting so I can face her and I can see the way she lifts her chin up that she wants me to kiss her, so I do.

It's too cold to do anything else. The fire helps a little, but we just kiss until my erection aches and then kiss some more. I don't even try to reach under her jacket though, as much as I want to. We stop when we hear the car return. They sound even more wasted than when they left and Sasha and I look at each other, relieved they returned okay.

"They're going to be drunk and stoned all night," I say.
"Yeah."
"Freezing out here. Think I'll get my ass home."
She says, "It's still early."
"Yeah. I didn't say I wanted to stay home," I tell her, smiling.
The three amigos are coming through the gate by this time. We sit around the fire and eat. Sasha and I aren't drinking and the others are too wasted to notice. But everyone gets cold and nobody wants to hang out with Mel's sister. Besides, Corbin and Jake are still trying to score weed. We spend a few more minutes and finally I really mean it when I say, "I'm freezing my balls off."

Everyone laughs and we all get up. Corbin, Jake, and I head toward the car, the girls walking behind us and they start giggling.

Jake says, "Every time!" and he's got a point. We all laugh.
When I get home the first thing I do is shower the stale smoke off, and brush my teeth and drink enough water to get rid of the foul remnants of that vodka. I sneak some better-quality stuff from my dad's bar, pouring just a little into an empty plastic water bottle.
Then I call Sasha.
"Hey."
"Hi."
"Think you can get out to the desert?"
"What's in the desert?"
"Me."
"Okay."

I get there before she does, sitting in my parked car. Headlights bounce into the parking area and I leave my engine running until I can tell it's her. I roll down my window so she can see me and she gets out and hops into my passenger seat. I'm glad she didn't bother with the jacket this time. She still smells like stale smoke from the fire, but I don't mind that much. I turn the engine off and pull out the water bottle with my dad's whiskey in it, thinking if she hasn't brushed her teeth then maybe we should at least have a few sips, just for the sake of mouthwash.

She says, "I'm driving."

"Me, too. Just a little sip. Keep us warm."

I take a drink and hand it to her. She has a small sip and says, "Ugh."

"Yeah. Better than that vile crap earlier though."

"I guess."

"You leave Mel with her sister?"

"Yeah. She couldn't leave her alone at home. They were both stoned and started arguing about shit. I didn't even know what. Stupid."

"Jake and Corbin are on a mission," I tell her.

She laughs at that. "Sometimes I think it's all they talk about."

"That and garden gnomes." Suddenly she leans over and plants her mouth on mine so firmly I feel her teeth for a moment and then we lock lips. This time I put my hand up her shirt and squeeze her through her bra. We continue like that for a while and I am right back at that stage, aching down there and wondering how long a girl can just keep kissing. I've had a hand on her ass for a while and try moving it between her legs. She spreads them for me, her jeans presenting a frustrating barrier for both of us.

I pull back and reach for the door handle.

She says, "Where are you going?"

"Backseat," I respond, "you coming?"

She is. When she gets in with me we have to start the kissing again, apparently. It's going to get cold quickly, though, and I'm at the point

I need to find out if we are going to go further or not. I reach for her bra strap and she lets me undo it. When my hands feel the skin of her boobs it brings me to the point I just can't wait any more. I squeeze one and feel the nipple and reach for the button on her jeans. I guess she's made up her mind, too, because she starts racing me to get them off and I don't need to make sure the panties go too because she beats me to it.

I reach between her legs and she spreads them. She is slick, and I rub her clitoris a bit, then start getting out of my own pants. I fumble in the pocket and pull out a condom, and when she grabs my penis I stop moving. It feels damn good. She grips me a little bit, and says, "Oh, put it on."

I am glad to, for all the regular reasons, but also because I think I might only last about five seconds if I don't. One thing about her being 5'2" is that she fits just fine in the backseat, and at this point I could be contorted into the shape of a pretzel and still figure out how to put it in. Even though I'm on top once again, the way we're having to fit in the backseat gives me a better view of the action than I usually get from missionary. In fact, it's not like usual at all, and when I put myself against her and start to go in, I'm able to watch. It feels warm and tight and I like seeing the reaction it gets from her.

I start to move in and out and I'm so turned on I really am having a tough time starting slowly at all. I push hard enough to move her and she puts her arms up over her head, against the door to push herself back against me. What that does to her chest is just right, and I lean over and suck on one of her nipples for a bit.

"Ohh," comes out of her mouth and I start flicking the nipple with my tongue, and she adds, "Oh, God."

The condom really does limit the sensation, but I'm having too damn much fun to care, and as I keep thrusting she starts getting this surprised look on her face. She moves her arms down to my hips and just holds on for the ride, and then she twists her whole face up, and for a second I think she's in pain or about to start crying, and then I realize she's coming like gangbusters, and that's all there is left in the equation for me as I lose it too.

We wait until things subside a bit. I'm wanting to play with her chest some more. It's staring me in the face. We kiss, but it's already cold again in the car and we get dressed fast. When we're moving back to the front I put the used condom and its wrapper in the only trashcan in the area. In some other place I might just leave it lying out there like a trophy or something, maybe, but not this close to my old middle school.

After that she started calling me every other day. We got together a few more times. Then one day she let me know she wanted to experiment a little bit, by trying out the sixty-nine position. Who was I to say no? She came over to my place. I don't remember any more if we picked a night when my parents weren't home, or if I snuck her in late, but we were in my room with the lights off. We got ourselves into position, kind of lying beside each other at first. She gripped me and took the tip of my penis into her mouth. It didn't feel bad at all, but it hadn't really started feeling all that good yet either, as I was still getting settled in and trying to figure out the awkward positioning with ol' garden gnome. I guess I call her that again in hindsight, because what came next put a big damn damper on the whole thing. Right as I was about to start "orally pleasuring" her I smelled something so foul I couldn't really make out what it was. But it sure crossed my eyes. I stopped everything, and told her I was not comfortable doing this with her. She was fully confused, and I didn't blame her but I did not have any intention of telling her what happened. I walked her back downstairs and we talked awkwardly for a bit. I cannot remember a single word of that conversation. Finally I went back up to my room and turned on the lights, and in no time discovered a small piece of poop sitting right on top of my bed. Yeah. The garden gnome was lacking in the wiping department. There are some details a guy just forgets, and I wish I could but never have forgotten that particular smell, nor discovering that little gem of a turd on my bed cover. She was gone and I never did try speaking with her again.

Penelope

As the summer neared an end Justin and I caught up with each other and started hanging out more. We found ourselves at the mall one day. I was thinking about a new pair of shoes and maybe some jeans, and checking out the games store without buying anything. Then we went to the bookstore, which, looking back, I realize had become one of my favorite places. Justin and I were browsing in different aisles when a group of girls came in. I think maybe at first I thought any girl I met in a bookstore might have a little extra going on, but without trying to give too much away let me say, just because someone likes a book now and again doesn't mean they're not an asshole.

We caught each other's eye enough so I figured she was about as interested as I was. She was cute, and taller than the lawn gnome.

"Hey," I say.
"Hi."
"I'm Daniel."
"Penelope," she reaches out her hand.
"What are you doing here?"
"Uh, book shopping."
"Yeah. Anything in particular?"
"Just summer reading I have to do for English. Boring. You'd think just once they could pick something a little fun. What about you?"
"Just browsing."
"Is that your friend?"
"Yeah, Justin."

"What do you guys do?"

"Hang out at my place mostly. We're night owls. Used to play games or get online all night, but I'm getting a little sick of that."

"My friends and I like to stay up late, too, but everything's so boring in my neighborhood."

"Where do you live?"

"Over on Escher."

"We're close. I'm only two miles away from there."

Before long she and some of her friends would sneak over. We had more room and my parents didn't pay much attention since we kept things quiet and they always arrived very late at night. Justin and I were surprised at first to meet a bunch of girls that liked staying up as late as we did.

Sometimes we'd all sneak out and go somewhere, but usually we just hung out talking, watching videos or movies online, sneaking some of my dad's booze.

It became apparent after a few visits that Penelope had a large group of friends, because it was often a different couple of girls joining her. One night Justin joked to me that he thought she picked which ones got to come along by how far they'd been able to shove their noses up her butt. I laughed so hard I just about hit the floor because we hadn't put our finger on it before and suddenly he pegged it. He had to be exactly right. The next time Penelope showed up, we both started chuckling, then giggling our asses off. There she was, and there was one girl with a familiar face and two new ones, and they were all kind of huddled behind her, bent over just a bit so you could almost draw a line from their noses to Penelope's rear end.

"What's so funny?"

"Nothing."
"Well, you're laughing. Something has to be funny."

I suddenly think it might be a little funny if someone slapped that look off her face, but just as quickly feel bad. Then, I have to admit, I think—instead of an actual smack—maybe I'll just go ahead and fuck that look off her face. A thought like that has never crossed my mind before, and it feels wrong while at the same time turning me on. I look at her face and the way she watches her gaggle of friends, like she is already angry and just ready and waiting to snap them into line, and then my mind lays over an image of how she'd look just before reaching orgasm. I feel it's almost my duty.

She's a little pissed. "You know it's not nice to zone out like that when someone is asking you a question."

This time I control the involuntary replay of a hand making contact with her cheek in my head, and the shocked look on her face before it spins around backwards. That's not me.

Finally I say, "You just had to be there."
She doesn't like the answer, but says, "We brought a Blu-Ray."

I offer to sneak some alcohol from my dad's bar and the girls gratefully accept. I get the impression they would have said no, except they're terrified of Penelope and would take anything that might help them have a good time.

I've learned my lesson about girls and whiskey, but there's this old barely-touched bottle of Southern Comfort in the back of the cabinet and I remember once at a party in the desert the girls seemed to hate it a little less than other stuff. I grab it and a couple of ginger ales.

Justin's so easygoing he's got the movie he and I would have never picked in a million years already going in my room. Between the bed, the chair, and the floor, everyone seems comfortable enough. After a few sips of alcohol the girls act a little less nervous, but Penelope is still in charge. She shushes anyone for talking during the movie, but then has no problem interrupting the lines herself. She seems to make a point of asking each of the girls some kind of personal question about something embarrassing that happened to them, making them agree how awful and stupid it was. This is a routine Justin and I have gotten used to.

Finally I say, "Hey, I wanted to ask you about something in private. Want to come to the living room for a sec?"
"No. I'm watching the movie."
I shrug, looking over at Justin. He's got his computer in his lap, happy as a clam surrounded by girls he doesn't have to talk to. I get up.
"Where are you going?"
"To get some ice."
I walk out, telling myself if she doesn't follow my ass in thirty seconds or less I'm kicking her out. Her friends will be welcome to stay if they like. She makes it with about two seconds to spare.
"Why did you ask to see me in private? That was embarrassing."
"Why?"
"Because my friends will think we're up to something. You shouldn't make it so obvious."
"What would you prefer I said?"
"You could have asked me to help you get some ice."
"I thought you might just send one of them, but I wanted you." I realize that was exactly the right thing to say, and congratulate myself for it. Her face goes from confused and pissy to approving, and then she smiles. She is pretty, maybe even beautiful, and it's my turn to be

confused because it never crossed my mind before that I could be turned on by the very thing that repulsed me about a girl.

She moves her hips forward, not quite bumping me, but bringing her lips close enough to my face to leave no doubt. We kiss. Dammit if she isn't good at it. Her tongue slides confidently and slickly right into my mouth and I do the same thing back to her. We forget everything else and start making out on the couch. I get so damned turned on I wonder when in my life I'm going to be with a girl who wants to get busy at the same time I do. It's not that I don't enjoy the kissing, because I really do. But a little corner of my mind that isn't fully into what we're doing is wondering whether I should point out to her something all girls might want to consider...the more we do this the shorter the even better part is going to last.

But something tells me if it's going to happen, it's damn sure going to have to be her idea. So we keep kissing and I don't even try to put my hands up her shirt. She's practically begging me to, heaving her chest against me and hooking her leg over mine, but I just keep concentrating on our steamy lip lock. She starts pushing her mouth against me so hard I finally realize that whoever came up with the phrase, "tonsil tennis," was being just about literal. She's now practically humping my knee through her jeans, so I finally oblige and shove my hand against her crotch before she has a chance to stop me. I rub hard against right where I think she should like it and she pulls her mouth off mine and gasps. She lies back against the couch and spreads her legs, but I don't reach for the button, or her shirt. I don't have any idea what it is that's telling me all this, but I am convinced she would let me play with her all night long, satisfying her completely, and leaving me high and dry. Whether she gives it up or not, I'll be damned if I'm going to play that game, at least not with her. So I keep rubbing her through her jeans and

I guess she gets the idea and finally makes a decision, because she says, "Ohhh, come on. Fuck me."

I stand up and pull out a condom. She starts to undo her jeans, so I kick off my shoes and pull my pants off fast. Then I help her peel hers down, pulling off her shoes. She doesn't reach for me, and it's a good thing because I'm a little too close. There's just enough moonlight coming in from the window that I think I see a flash of reflection between her legs. It's enough to drive me even crazier.

I say, "Damn, I can see how wet you are."

I think she wants to try to stop me, but she's almost shaking. I rip open the condom wrapper and put it on, then I move to her and she hesitates for less than a second before spreading her legs wide and wrapping them around me as I move in. I'm sure of it now, she was going to stop it right then and see if she could dangle me for a while. I almost say out loud, "It's too late now, Penelope." But I'm in pretty much the same state she is, and as much as that would be legendary, I just don't want to blow it at this point.

I grab her ass and slide right in and she gasps. No girl I've been with before has come so fast. I can feel it even through the rubber and she's holding onto me for dear life, trying to keep from waking my parents. I'm worried she's done, but she takes a breath and says almost like before, "Oh, fuck me."

The pause is a good thing. Also the worry that I was about to have to stop right then. And she is so slick even with the rubber it feels almost like flesh on flesh. I concentrate on staying slow for a while, and reward myself by looking down and watching. It's a hell of a thing to see…not checking out one of a million bored porn stars faking things on screen, but actually watching yourself live in the moonlight. She starts to watch, too, and I grab her hand and put it down there so she can feel it happening. I must be on a roll, because that apparently was also a good idea. She whispers, "Oh, fffuck," and starts to buck her hips again. I finally stop trying to hold out and that's my last good play before the game is over, because I just let myself go and fuck her as hard as I can, as hard as I imagined earlier when thinking how much she needed someone to shut her up, and she actually shoves her forearm right into her open mouth to keep from screaming. It pissed me off she got off twice to my one time, but only a little.

We went back to my room, with ice. Justin looked up and I guess there was no hiding it because he gave me this huge grin. Penelope ignores it and the girls are too afraid of her to let fly with the giggles. Instead they look at each other wide-eyed. She goes back to the same spot she was in before like nothing happened, and I find my glass and take myself a drink.

Later that night, after they'd gone, I told him about it. He laughed the whole time as I detailed what was going on in my head.

He said, "So that's what angry sex is, huh? Doesn't sound bad."

I laughed. And he was right. If I could have, I would have gone to her house that night for round two.

But she kept coming over, and kept rotating her friends like accessories in whatever punishment and reward system she'd worked out. Justin just went with the flow. He never did hook up with any of them. I think he didn't like what a controlling bitch she was, and he didn't like anyone who'd let someone else control them, either. And he kind of fumbled all over himself still when talking with girls. I still did too, with some of them.

Even with Penelope, every time she came over, if I acted too eager, or let myself fall into the trap of touching her, or even going down on her, before I'd had my fun, she'd leave me hanging every time. Sometimes she'd bring over some friends who weren't so petrified they couldn't talk, and I swear she stared at me angrily if I said more than two words to any of them. I joked with Justin one time, if she could make her perfect world, everyone in it would have a slot in the back of their heads so Penelope could stick her hand in, and work every conversation around her exactly the way it was supposed to go, by making all the puppets talk.

One time we were at the mall again and I was talking with a girl I knew from school. I mean, of course I was interested in her, but we were just chatting about people we knew when Penelope marched up and spat right out, "So who's this?"

The other girl scoffed and said, "Whatever," but walked away while Penelope burned holes in her back. And I never did actually date Penelope. I mean the idea of taking her out and buying her a dinner, and then sitting through it while she stared at my mouth, waiting to pounce the instant it made a mistake, well, no sex, angry or otherwise, was worth that to me. She acted like a supermodel who woke up one day to find out she'd been made the Queen of England. And believe me, she didn't have a royal drop of blood in her, and she was no model. Before school even started I stopped talking to her.

Anna

Justin and I were still hanging out. He had started being up for going out a little more often. There was a burger joint in town a lot of kids from our high school went to and we were there one afternoon. Justin and I were talking, it could have been about literally anything, when I heard this high-pitched voice that made everyone else in the place sound like they were murmuring low. It wasn't a bad sound, not at all, or maybe I just thought that after I saw her. She could not have been more my type: brunette with blue eyes and this killer tight body and enough in the chest to make her t-shirt strain. Justin stopped and turned, and I won't lie, I could almost have kissed him when he waved to one of the friends this girl was with.

They came over.

"Hi, Justin."
"Hey. What are you up to?"
"Just getting something to eat."
"Yeah, what was that in the cafeteria today?"
"I know!"
"This is Daniel," he said.
"Hi, this is Anna."

She said hello and I still remember it sounding like the high notes on a piano. We ended up sitting together and eating and I learned she lived in the same neighborhood as Jen. Even after all that time, and seeing this gorgeous new girl with the high-pitched voice that was oddly turning me on, thinking about Jen's neighborhood brought back a fast slideshow of images. I saw her house exactly the way it looked when we used to sneak kisses, and the park, and the sidewalks late at night when I was desperate enough to walk so many miles for her. I hated to admit it to myself back then that it could all still get to me, and I hate to admit it now. I can still smell the fucking grass in all those front yards I passed, cold and soaked with dew.

But I guess I let it all fly by in a way that wasn't obvious, because we chatted and ate our burgers, and I am telling you it was not easy to keep from staring at Anna's blue eyes, which looked like a cat's peering out from the frame of her dark hair.

Later that same week the four of us met up at the movie theater. I couldn't tell you which one because all I could think about was getting out of there and moving things forward with Anna. And if I've been giving the impression all I had was one thing on my mind, well, that's true and it's not. I mean, it's absolutely one-hundred percent true. I was a teenage male. But I was all for something real. It's just that the first time something real happened for me my heart got squished like a tire hitting a jelly donut. I tell myself I was too young, and so was she, and we got so intense that it was all too much. Jen and I talked about growing old together, if you can believe that.

And then? Well, whatever it was Lisa and I had we were both aiming at Jen for our own reasons. After that I find a turd in my bed from a garden gnome.

Then I move on to get together with a real turd of a human being, and I think the part of my brain that was open for something more than just a sexual relationship was already so gun-shy by that time it figured the best thing to do was just get the hell out of the way and hope. And sitting there in that movie theatre with my friend and these two girls, I did hope. But I also wanted to get a move on.

I think she did, too. Later that same week we met up at a party. It was at someone's house her friend knew. Parties were starting to change a little bit. I mean not all that much, but even a year makes a big difference when you're younger than 20. And what I noticed was that there was less of a full-on commotion when a guy and a girl were one-on-one. Don't get me wrong, there were looks and maybe even giggles, and a little good-natured ribbing, but it no longer hit like a grenade going off in a crowded room. So Anna and I drank together and she told me more about herself. I learned about her little brother, and her parents, and that she got good grades and was thinking about college but didn't have the first clue what she wanted to study. None of it was making the earth move, but I listened to her stories and enjoyed the way her voice kept making everyone else, even girls, sound like jolly green giants. And, yeah, I kept fantasizing about hearing it moaning in my ear. I mean, if it was that high when she spoke normally, what kind of falsetto did she have in her?

I told her about me, too, although I avoided the subject of other girls. I wonder sometimes if we're all crazy when it comes to that. Because, I mean unless you're one of those lucky people who figured out what they wanted to do with themselves from the age of five, it can be hard to define anything about ourselves without talking about who we've loved, or at least in terms of high school, been with. Right? Hell, I don't know. But I know the last thing I want to hear about from a woman I'm with is who they've been with and how they loved and why it's over. And if you couldn't tell already, I learned pretty early that girls feel exactly the same way. It's a hell of a way to start out, hiding who we are from each other.

So Anna didn't get in very deep, but I guess it was far enough. Because after a few more parties and nights out drinking she brought me to her house.

Her parents are out, not even coming back tonight. It hits me that even with all the liberty my parents have given me as I've been getting older that it's pretty unusual to be in a warm house all alone with a girl. We're shushing each other and giggling for no reason, and I point it out.

"You're right," she says in that pitch that makes me wonder if I was actually wrong, because it might be piercing the walls into the neighbors' bedrooms. But there is no time to bother about it further, because she is on a mission. She has my hand and has already pulled me to her room and doesn't let me go until we are actually lying on her bed together. I'm not about to complain.

And the only thing I do wonder is if I should pull out my phone and note the date, because for once the kissing doesn't go on forever. She gets us naked and under the covers and before I even have a chance to put my hands on her boobs the way I've been wanting to for weeks she pulls one down right between her legs. There is nothing like the feeling of a girl who has been ready for a while. There is no hunting for moisture or foreplay on the clitoris, because she's already slick and warm and spread. So I do the only thing I can, and slip a finger inside while sucking on one of her perfect little nipples. Damn, if I wasn't right. Her voice reaches a register I can barely hear, and I have to keep myself from laughing as I imagine the dogs of the neighborhood starting up and running for shelter.

I finger-bang her and she moans in rhythm and I feel her pulses squeezing my hand in less than a minute. It just makes her hornier. She doesn't have the first clue what she's doing, but she's trying to be sexy. I'm almost tempted to tell her she's so hot she doesn't have to try anything but whatever feels good, but I don't want to embarrass her and decide to just enjoy being her toy.

She pumps me with her hand a bit and then goes down on me. She sort of holds the tip in her mouth and doesn't really move, and it drives me crazy. I want to put my hand on her head and push her down but it somehow feels wrong. Damn. If she knew what she was doing…I start fantasizing about her going deeper and rubbing my balls a bit and the whole time I'm already in her mouth. It's weird, but fun as hell.

Then she climbs up on me at last. She sits down on me awkwardly and I have to reach and adjust so I can try to get inside her. As wet as she is, it's difficult. It's like she's all clenched up, and she says, "I'm nervous."
"We can do anything you like," I tell her.

This seems to make her comfortable, because although it's still some effort she stops being shy about it and grabs me and puts it right at the entrance to her pussy.

I say, "I just want to watch for a bit."
"Okay," she says. So I move my hands out of the way and she keeps aiming me in, and starts sitting a little lower. I'm watching this girl with the blue eyes and brunette hair, and her great tits and perfect little bush slowly working down on me and I'm about to lose it when I realize I haven't put anything on yet.
I say, "We forgot protection."
She says, "I just want to feel you inside me for a bit. Then you can put it on."
I know it's stupid, but I say, "Okay."

She keeps pressing me in and suddenly the feeling goes from this weird struggle to perfection. I don't really know for sure, but I think she was so clenched there was actually a bone inside of her blocking things, because I feel something hard release and move out of the way. And she moans again and starts grinding against me and I am sorry, but there is no way I'm stopping anything. She slides up and down and grinds—and when she grinds she gasps and her mouth opens—and I am just about to lose it when she stops and says, "Take me from behind, okay?"

I fumble for the condom as she gets on her hands and knees and she says, "Oh, just stick it in. I want to feel you from behind."

And I've got no sense left anyway, so I oblige. She doesn't really know what to do and has her back hunched the wrong way, but she's moaning and saying "Oh, oh, oh," every time I push and then she starts to shake like she doesn't know what the hell is happening to her. And then I just pull her hips as hard as I can against me and let it go as deep inside her as I can get, and she's shaking even more and I feel her pulsing. I'm making some pretty good noise myself by this point and she's even louder with the "Oh, OH, OH," and I start to wonder if she's ever going to stop.

Finally she does, and she says, "Wow. I came twice like that."

That's a first in my experience and I don't even want to say what I'm thinking because I don't want to spoil it for her, but I have to. "I came, too, without protection."

She contemplates this for a bit and then says, "Oh, well. Too late now." And she shrugs. For the rest of the night, I fully acquiesce. I let her try everything she wants. She doesn't ask me once if she's doing things right or not and I don't bother bringing it up either. It's about the most fun I've ever had.

Two weeks later she had her period, and I stopped sweating morning, noon, and night. She didn't call me after that for a while, and I didn't call her either. Maybe I sensed something, but I doubt it. I think it was more that we dodged a bullet and I didn't know how the hell we were going to top that night. That, and as much as her voice had been turning me on, I wasn't all that ready to hear it again too soon. I'm not proud of that, but there it is.

And before anyone thinks I'm the asshole, let me tell you what I found out. Justin and I went out to a party and there were these two girls giggling their asses off every time we walked by.

Finally I said, "You gonna tell me what's so funny or just keep acting like idiots?" But I said it with a smile.

The two girls looked at each other. I guess they were trying to decide whether to act offended or not. But we all knew they had something to get off their chests, and one of them said, "You're going with Anna, right?"
"No."
"Well that's good for you, then."
"Why?"
"Because I know for a fact she's having sex with her sister's boyfriend." I acted like a one-man audience, giving her a little applause like she'd won the prize for worst person of the day, then walked away. But I won't deny I was pissed. I didn't even want to admit it to myself, but I told Justin about it. He did a little checking for me and it turned out to be true. I guess the argument Anna had one day with her sister in the middle of school in front of everybody turned out to become a mini-legend.

And that was one more I chalked up, and I'm not talking about keeping score. More like a confirmation of what I thought I'd already learned about girls. Hell, this was one more I never actually dated. Meeting up at the movies and paying for our own food when we got together is different. She didn't owe me shit and I had a ball, and we never talked again either.

Thinking about Anna, collected my thoughts in my dark room where I no longer felt the need to be with someone. However, nights became lonely fast. I began to drink more and started smoking cigarettes. I wrote down in a brown journal that I had kept of all the experiences with the women that I have had. All of the thoughts that came to my mind and how I felt afterwards.

I kept quiet from my friends keeping communication short with them. I wanted more from women but decided it wasn't serving me any good. "What if I catch AIDS?" I think to myself. "Or herpes?"
"Fuck…"

I knew that my sexual drive had to be calmed and that I have been immature about handling these situations with women. Even though with Anna, who decided to keep me as a "side-dick" I still had some emotional desire to be with them. I wanted them to be with me and only me.

As nights alone went on for about a week or two I had stayed up late to speak with my mother who was getting ready for work that morning. The sun was rising and I had been up all through the night smoking and drinking my dad's whiskey.

"Mom.."
She reaches a glass in our kitchen cabinet and has a look of surprise on her face.
"You're awake?" She asks me.
"No I stayed up all night.." I tell her.
"You need to sleep.. get your sleep schedule back in order."

"I know." I tell her.

She quickly grabs her bag and heads out the garage to her car.

My mother and I didn't have a close relationship. But she could tell what I was doing wrong with my life and the women I have been with. Multiple times I could hear the small footsteps in my parent's room and acute noises knowing that she was listening. My parents didn't even sleep in the same bedroom. My father snored clamorously as if an elephant was snoozing in our house and my mother slept in my sister's old bedroom when she left the house for college. I didn't feel I could rely on my mom or especially my father for any kind of emotional support.

I knew my problem… I wanted to gain that from the women that I have been with and wanted them to listen to my problems and emotions. Things I wanted to talk about.

Eventually, getting tired of the same routine of being alone at night I decided to stay away from women and focus on myself and school that my parents have been concerned with. I met up with Justin late day, we went to the mall and browsed through the bookstore. He asked me questions of how I have been doing. I don't remember too much of what we talked about. Later as it got late, I walked outside the bookstore and saw two boys and a very tall girl sitting on a curb outside of the bookstore laughing.

As we walk past them the very tall girl speaks to us.

"Hey, you guys want to see us prank call the White House?" She says. How could I refuse that? Hell, who prank calls the White House? Sounded too good to be true.

"Sure." I tell her smiling.

The two boys end up calling them a number which actually directed it to a representative of the White House. (Anyone can get that number) He starts talking crap about the current president and food stamps and hangs up. I can't recollect exactly how that went.

I noticed the boy talking on the phone someone who went to the charter school that I had transferred to.

I look at him.

"Hey man… where have I seen you before?" I ask him.

"You went to…" He says cutting himself off smiling.

"Yeah… I didn't talk to many people there." I tell him.

Later that evening I had asked them what they were up to. It appeared that they were also late nighters. I thought at the time that they would become close friends. I was right. Two of them did.

Luke & Tracy.

After meeting them the other guy was someone who appeared to only be there temporarily. I don't remember his name. And I couldn't even recollect why he was there with them. My nights alone became nights with friends who stayed up late with me. We all spoke with each other over social media and met up late at night in the darkest hours 'til twilight.

After the mall was closed we would meet in a specific area in the parking lot to meet up at night. Luke or Tracy would pick me up. And we would have ourselves a good time. Sometimes drinking in my backyard or sitting in one car blaring music in a secluded area in the mall parking lot. We developed close friendships with each other. We were inseparable.

Luke and I became the closest, I viewed him like a younger brother, though he was taller than me, had whiter skin, and a goofy laugh.

🐇 Caitlyn 🐇

Summer began to warm the air. The asphalt would grow hot and clouds were desired going outside during the day. I haven't spoke much with Justin as our friendship decreased and he moved onto another group of friends. Luke and I have been going to our bookstore to meet with Tracy and a few other people who we would meet from time to time.

"Hey man what are we doing tonight?" Luke asks me picking me up from the front of my house.

"Uhm, I don't know, man, same thing." I tell him jumping in his car and lighting a cigarette.

"Alright alright," Luke says to me as we drive off.

I look at the backseat of his vehicle and see a case of really cheap beer that had about 15-20 beers left inside of it.

"Why do you have that?" I ask him.

"No idea, that beer tastes like shit. Got it from my stepdad."

Luke rolled down his window at a stoplight in a left turn lane. There was a homeless man with newspapers in the median.

"Hey man, you want some beer?" Luke shouts out from his car window.

"Yeah, I'll take a beer." He says.

Luke reached for the case of beer that was sitting in his backseat and hands him the entire box.

"God bless you." The homeless man says and walks back to sit at the median with his newspapers.

"You're weird, man," I tell Luke, laughing that he just gave a homeless man a few beers.

"So, I have to ask you something." Luke says.

"Ask away."

"So you remember Caitlyn right?"

"Yeah, you still talk to her or she still has a thing for you?" I turn to him while I light a cigarette.

"We don't have a thing."

"Okay so what about her?"

Luke starts to smile at me and begins laughing.

"Are you two fucking?" I ask him.

"Yes BUT... I needed to ask you something."

"Fuck man just ask." My eyes open trying to fork out whatever it was that Luke really wanted to ask or know.

"She wants to have a threesome."

I start coughing and throw my cigarette out of the window. Luke continued to drive and kept smiling, looking at me then, the road... me, and then the road.

"Well?" He asks shifting his car.

"Should you do it?" I ask looking at him. "With who?"

"Uhm.. What do you think I'm asking you for?" Luke says still smiling. I begin to nod my head repeatedly. "NO NO FUCK NO, I don't want to see your dick man."

"C'mon we don't have to look at each other."

"Are you fucking kidding me man? That is so so weird." I tell him.

"Ok, just think about it." He says with a shit grin on his face.

Luke did not bring it up again for a while. We still spent time at my house watching T.V. during the dark hours of the night and having a drink and smoking a cigarette or two in the backyard. We did this for many of the summer months where nights outside felt perfect. However, the more I got to know Luke, the more I saw how much of a little bull-shitter he was. Not in a malicious way, but he enjoyed being young and fucking around, experimenting with everything he could. In some ways he was like me. I accepted it and decided to give in.

I remember Luke and me sitting on my back patio one night, drunk. I can't remember much about that conversation.

"Alright man." I look at him and point my cigarette at him. "If you get that girl over here, we will... see what happens." I tell him.
Luke clapped his hands together and smiled with that shit grin.
"Really?" Luke says as he starts to laugh.
"Do you know what she wants to do?" I ask him
"Nope—all I know is that she wants a threesome."

Friday approached quickly and I haven't heard anything about this threesome with Caitlyn. Details did not arrive and I had no idea if this thing was going to happen. I didn't worry too much about it and didn't really care if it didn't. I spent that day with Luke and Tracy, drinking coffee outside of our bookstore and smoking cigarettes which by now I was addicted to. I breathed in the smoke easily.

"We hanging out tonight?" Tracy asks sipping on her coffee.
"Daniel and I have things to do tonight." Luke replies to her.
"What are you two doing?" She asks.
Luke looks at me and begins rocking back and forth in his chair smiling at me.
"What is that shit grin for?" I ask smiling back at him.
"You know." He says exhaling his cigarette.
Tracy looks at Luke then me.
"Gay." She states.
Luke and I both start laughing.
"Do I even want to know?" Tracy asks with a puzzling face.
"Is it? What I think it is?" I ask Luke.
"Yep. We're doing it." He says to me. "Tracy, we will tell you later," he adds.
"Sounds like you two are fucking each other," she tells us, laughing.

"Something like that," Luke says laughing.

"Well that's enough for me." Tracy says rolling her eyes and standing up. "I'm out of here. Let me know if you two aren't being gay," she says, walking off to her car.

Later that evening Luke invites me over to his place. His stepfather was out of town and his mother worked at night. Which made the worry of parents gratuitous.

"Alright man so here are some rules." Luke says.

"Okay?"

"No touching my balls, or anything."

"Dude, you don't have to tell me twice." I tell him. "I won't even look at you." I say.

"Okay." Luke says with that shit grin that I wished didn't exist.

I played on Luke's parents' pool table as he left the house for a while. Sipping on a beer, I thought to myself.

"There's no way. He has got to be bull-shitting."

A few minutes go by and I hear the front door open. Luke and Caitlyn walk in.

As soon as I saw her I thought to myself again. "Oh fuck, we're doing this."

Caitlyn was slim but curvy. She has dark hair that went to her shoulders and appeared to be more mature than most girls I have talked to before. She was an acquaintance through Tracy and Luke and the only times I had talked to her was when I was with them and she happened to be around. I didn't care too much about her or any other woman since I decided to stay away from them, or any other sexual desires.

My mind became a film strip of pictures of perverted thoughts with this girl. This felt different because of my friend Luke being included in my periphery as well. My abundance of the situation left feelings of elation and chagrin. However, her confidence was most profound.

"Daniel," Luke says as I strike a pool ball.
"Yep." I say looking at him across the room.
"Come over here man." He says.

I walk around and see Luke and Caitlyn sitting on the couch. I don't sit next to Luke and place myself to Caitlyn. Having her sit in between us.

"So how do you want to do this?" he asks her.

I guessed there would be a few loose ends. Caitlyn being shy or nervous. She knew exactly what she was doing. Exactly what she wanted.

Caitlyn didn't hesitate to answer. She didn't appear to act awkward or overtly promiscuous. Her confidence was, again, impressive.

"I want this to be even." She says looking at Luke then at myself.
"What do you mean?" Luke asks her.
"Just even. Don't know a better way to describe it." She says giggling.
"Well, I don't want Daniel's balls touching mine." Luke says looking at her then myself.
"I second that." I say.
"That's fine," she says, laughing.

Caitlyn took both of her hands and reached down in our pants. It was almost difficult for me to obtain an erection. I was veraciously astonished with her attitude. She began to undo my belt, and began sucking on me. Keeping Luke in her other hand. She went back and forth for a while. Thoughts I had during this time I was telling myself, "Dude, I have Luke's dick germs on me." I wanted to laugh a few times but kept focus on what we were doing.

Caitlyn got on top of Luke while sitting on the couch, and I stood up from the couch and allowed her to continue sucking on me. She appeared to be having a good time. I brushed my hands through her hair into a ponytail, and began fucking her mouth. She was incredibly experienced, letting us do whatever we wanted with her. I pushed myself deep into her mouth while her eyes stared straight at me. Luke picked her up. Caitlyn got on her hands and knees while Luke entered behind her. She let out a loud moan with my cock in her mouth and looked behind her to Luke.

"Harder, harder," she says.

I start, to move around a bit in her mouth. Pressing on the inside of her cheek. Her eyes squint at me and starts to suck on my balls.
"You taste so fucking good," she says, and puts my cock back in her mouth.

Luke grabbed her hair, and began to pull on it. Obviously having a dick in her mouth at this time would be difficult. I began to lightly slap her face with my cock. She began moaning and grabbed onto my thigh.
"More… more," she says.

Luke let go of her hair and she began sucking on me again. Just on the side of my periphery, I could see Luke smiling. I didn't want to make eye contact with him but I did. And he held up one hand for a high five. I shook my head, and continued to allow Caitlyn to do her thing with us.

"Cum on my ass," she says, turning back to Luke.

Luke, began speeding up a bit while she continued to shove my entire penis down her throat. I won't lie. I felt extremely awkward. But if it's what she wanted… I didn't refuse to fuck her mouth as hard as I could. I wanted to also cum, but felt an awkwardness if it was before Luke. "Do I just walk away afterwards?" I tell myself.

Luke, pulled out, removed the condom he had on, and came right on her ass. He stopped, got up and walked to the bathroom. Caitlyn placed herself on her knees and began stroking me and staring at me with that squint.

"You want to come in my mouth?" She asks me.
I murmur "yes."
A minute or two later I had to groan a little bit myself.
"I'm going to cum." I tell her.
She shoves myself all the way down her throat and lets me cum.
"Holy. Shit." I tell myself.
She continues to suck on me even though I just came. As soon as she stops she looks up at me and starts smiling. Then, laughs.
"The fuck," I think to myself.

I awkwardly leave the room to the bathroom to wash up. As I turned on his bathtub, I could see his reflection through the bathroom mirror quietly giggling. I look at him and smile back.

"Dude…" I say to him nodding my head. "She's crazy."
"Nah." Luke tells me. "No crazier than either you or I."
"True," I reply.

I didn't want to go back downstairs and have an awkward after-threesome conversation. I got in the bath and relaxed for a second thinking about what I just did.

"Fuck, man." I told myself laying there in the bath.

I hopped out after 20 minutes and dressed myself. I looked around my genital area to make sure there was nothing wrong or any damage done.

"Okay, looks good." I reassure myself.

I walked downstairs and looked at the couch where I was just at. I sat on a far end of the sectional and turned on the television.

"This couch is tainted." I tell myself.

I wait for Luke to come through the front door, and tune into some wildlife show. I couldn't even pay attention to anything that was coming out of the T.V. I kept laughing and giggling to myself. If anyone saw me they probably would've thought I was crazy.

I heard the door open and looked behind the couch to ensure it was Luke coming through the door. He quickly closed the door behind him and ran over.

"Dude," he says looking at me laughing.

I run my hands through my hair and stare at the television.

"I can't look at you the same way." I tell him jokingly.

Luke begins to laugh and walks into the kitchen.

"Hey, what did she say to you when you took her home?" I ask him.

"Nothing really," he tells me, holding a box of pizza rolls. "You want a few?" He asks.

"Sure." I tell him.

"She said she had fun!" Luke shouts from the kitchen.

I nod my head and look back from the couch. "Yeah, this couch needs to be set on fire now." I tell him.

Luke began to laugh. "Eh, pretty sure my parents have sex on this thing all the time when I'm not home."

"Dude gross." I say to him.

"She kissed me on the cheek before I dropped her off." Luke mentions. "Good for her."

For the rest of the evening Luke and I watched random television shows and ended up passing out on that tainted sectional. Thankfully, it didn't smell bad and it wasn't stained. However, I thought that if the couch had feelings it would've been yelling at us to chill out the entire time. I didn't look at Luke differently at all. And to this day we still see each other and laugh about it.

Days after we would still see Caitlyn at the bookstore or passing by in restaurants   and parties. She didn't act awkward and always greeted us when we walked by. Shortly following she disappeared and she was never brought up again. She was another woman of the past who I deeply respected for her show of confidence. I had a good time and I'm glad she did as well. Efforts to do it again weren't desirable.

Luke and I remained close friends, and we were able to catch Tracy the day after the great trio on that tainted sectional. We met up at Tracy's place and threw back a few beers.

"So you buys want to mention what you two were being so odd about the other day?" She asks.

Luke and I look at each other and burst with laughter.

"Uh...." Luke says trying to hold in his laughter. "Daniel, can I tell her?" He asks.

"I don't care, man." I tell him. "It is what it is."

Luke explained the story to Tracy. There, I counted multiple times of her jaw dropping over and over. Her pupils dilated in disbelief.

"**WHAT!?**" Tracy started to squish her face with her hands.

"Daniel, Luke, bad. That's bad."

"Well she wanted to do it." Luke says to her.

"I had math class with that girl!" Tracy tells us as she opens another beer. "I've known her for quite some time." She added.

Luke and I laughed until our faces were red. I remember that night I laughed so hard that it felt like a while since I couldn't catch my breath off of something I found so hysterical. And when I mean hysterical, I mean it by the look of Tracy's face.

"Gross!" She says smiling and shaking her head. "I can't believe you two!"

Tracy was like one of the guys. She was the best girlfriend I had. She also felt like an older sister to me. Someone who I could talk to about a girl if there was ever any issues I wanted to discuss.

"You boys should get yourselves checked." She tells us.

"There is no way we have something." I tell her.

Tracy laughs and puts her beer on the table and points at me.

"Right, but she could've!" She says with laughter. "If she was that easy... think about it." She adds.

"You're getting me all paranoid," I tell her.

"Good! Get yourself checked."

I let out a sigh and the laughter died down. Luke and I would chuckle every minute or so watching Tracy make facial expressions of disgust and disbelief. It didn't seem to leave her mind that night. However, I took Tracy's words seriously and planned to get an STD check and make sure I was okay. She made me so paranoid that I had thought to myself again, "I need to calm down with this shit."

For the rest of the evening we didn't bring up Caitlyn. We talked about the time left in the summer and made plans which weren't about school, or where we would travel. Hell, we didn't talk about where we wanted to go next or what we wanted to do a year from now. We talked about what we wanted to do in college and looked forward to the years of burgeoning adulthood. I enjoyed these conversations and felt at home with these two friends that I had. Corbin, Jake and Justin never reconciled our close friendships. And just like most friendships, we don't need to talk every day. We established memories together that will forever exist while we are living. Time was something that created those past friendships. And within time they will always exist but will not always be present. The space I had in my heart for them is always there, if they ever need me I'll come to them.

Emma

August. I remember the leaves' green color slowly fading. The air was fresh and crisp, and summer was preparing to make its exit soon. Tracy and Luke stayed close throughout summer. I had made plans to meet up with Tracy late at night to go see a boy she was dating at the time. Tracy had a new boyfriend every other month. Though I couldn't blame her for dating guys that were more sensitive than her. Tracy was, again, like us guys. But her dating choices were piss poor…. She would even admit that.

I receive a phone call and head downstairs. My house was dark, and at this time my parents knew I was leaving the house late at night. But they never said anything to me. I walk out the front door and lock it. I see Tracy parked right outside my house.

"Hey," I say to her getting in the car.
"You ready, dude?"
"Yeah, where are we going again?" I ask her.
"Richie moved to a new apartment… it's uh… down by Plantation Drive," she tells me.
"Fuck, that's pretty far," I tell her.
"It's not that bad. We'll shoot down the interstate," she tells me.
"Okay." I say. "Isn't this the guy who was crying over the phone because you told him you couldn't see him last week?" I ask.
"Yep."
"Jesus Christ, Tracy," I say letting out a short laugh.

We drove on the interstate downtown for about 20 minutes. As soon as we pulled into the apartment complex, it appeared that mostly college students stayed there. It was near the university and you could see students drinking outside on their balconies.

"There's a fuck-ton of people here," I say.
"Yep," Tracy quickly says.
"Is this a party?" I ask her.
"Yep."

I thought for a second looking around at all these college kids running around. I was 17 and thought how everyone here is most likely going to be older than I am.

"Is this guy in college as well?" I ask.
"Yep."
"Why are you so short tonight?" I ask her.
"Well, I'm not dating this guy because I like him," she tells me.
"So only to go to parties?" I ask her.
"Penis and Parties," she says.
"You're so awesome," I tell her laughing. "Using that vagina power." I add.
"Yep." Tracy says.

We pull into covered parking. Walking from there, we searched the complex for the apartment. There was a group of people outside on a balcony smoking and drinking. The front door was swung open. Tracy and I walked in.

There were so many people in such a small space. There was a bare couch in the living room and nothing else. I followed behind Tracy. "Richie," she says, smiling and holding her arms out.

Richie had black socks that went right to his shins. He wore his hat backwards and just looked like a tool. I guess it's what Tracy was into, but I didn't blurt my thoughts out of my mouth.

"Richie, this is my friend Daniel," she said.He placed his hand out and smiled at me.
"Hey man, nice to meet you."
"You too," I tell him smiling.

He came off as a nice guy and very likeable. He checked up on me through the night to see if I had a beer in my hand. Not only did he appear like a gentlemen, but he acted like one too.

"Daniel, come over here man." Richie said as he walked down into a hall in his apartment.
"I keep a cooler in here, so if you want something feel free."
"I appreciate that." I tell him.

I saw students come into the apartment and leave. Mostly looking for free beer and moving on to the next apartment building for other parties going on, I thought to myself.

"Dude college kids are fucking assholes. Looking for free beer."
Tracy continued to talk to Richie for what appeared to be a few hours now. I decided I would try to be social and talk with a few of the students and random people that were walking around the apartment. I walked over to Tracy and Richie who were standing in the kitchen kissing each other.

"Hey you two." I say.
"Daniel!" They both say, obviously intoxicated.
I laughed and placed my hand on my forehead.

"I'm uh, going to wander around the complex a bit."

"Okay. Is everything okay?" Tracy asked me.

"Yeah! Of course! I'm just going to be social and explore a bit." I tell her.

As soon as I walked outside of the apartment Tracy grabbed me by my shoulder.

"Is everything alright?" She asked again.

"Yes. Tracy!" I say laughing.

"Okay, because we can leave if you want."

"No! You're fine Tracy. Have fun." I tell her. "I'll be back I just want to look around I'll be back." I promise.

"Okay, call me if you need anything." She tells me.

I walk to another apartment and see a strobe light in one apartment with students smoking and drinking on the balcony. I decided, hell why not? Let's see if I can just walk in there.

The door was open, and there were girls and douchebag-looking guys everywhere. I couldn't believe how many guys wore their hats backwards and wore plaid shorts with long Nike tube socks.

There were different-colored lights being flashed everywhere and music that contained no lyrics, mostly techno or electronica. The apartment would've been an epileptic's worst nightmare. I decided to observe, not knowing how to talk to these drunken party-goers. I stepped outside to a clustered balcony and decided to light a cigarette with a beer in my hand.

"Hey, do you have a lighter?" Someone says, touching my shoulder.

I look to my side and see a girl in jeans and an olive shirt. She had green eyes and her hair was a chestnut brown.

"Yeah" I say reaching into my pocket.

"Thank you." She replies as I hand it to her.

"Yep." I say taking it back and returning it into my pocket.

"I've never seen you here before." She tells me.

I continue to look inside and watch these students just stand around the apartment and drink. I didn't look directly at her when I spoke.

"I actually just, walked over here from that apartment over there." I tell her pointing at Richie's apartment.

I turned around and leaned on the metal gate that aligned with the balcony. I didn't try to talk with her, and I most certainly wasn't on a mission to bond with someone.

She moved right next me with her cigarette and looked right at me.

"So you just walked in then?"

"Yeah pretty much." I tell her smiling avoiding eye contact.

"Me too." She tells me, laughing. "Well I came with friends, I think there are a few people they know here." She continued.

"This music and lights are killing me. I think I'm going to check out a couple other noisy neighbors." I tell her flicking my cigarette into the rocks.

"Okay," She says. "I'm Emma by the way," She adds.

"Nice to meet you." I say shaking her hand.

I hopped the fence and walked towards Richie's apartment. Only a half hour went by until three girls walked in, one being Emma. I laughed to myself and struck a thought of where Tracy was. I began to look around the apartment and knocked on Richie's bedroom door. After a few attempts at knocking politely I knocked on it a little louder. I stuck my mouth close to where the doorknob was.

"Tracy!" I yelled through the door crack.

I received a text message shortly after.

"Sex. I'm OK."

I shook my head and poured beer from a keg that was standing in the kitchen. Emma approached me.

"Hey again." She says as I fill up my red cup.

"Hey!" I say smiling.

"Is this another random place you're at?" She asks.

"No, My friends are doing something in that room over there." I say pointing at the door.

"What, are they fucking?" She says laughing.

"I don't know," I tell her. "I'm going to walk around a bit." I add.

"Can I come with you?" She asked me. "I can't stand being around all this noise."

"Sure." I tell her.

"I need to get cigarettes out of my car anyway." She says.

As I begin to walk out of the door she lightly pulls on my shirt and looks back.

"Hold on a second." She says.

Emma made a few hand gestures towards the other two girls that walked in with her. One of them couldn't understand what she was trying to tell them, and walked up to her. Emma spoke directly into her ear as her friend looked right at me. She shook her head and Emma walked back up to me.

"Okay-- I had to let them know!" She said.

Emma and I walked around the complex. We looked at other parties going on and smoked a few cigarettes. I can't remember much of what we talked about. She was a college student who was two years older than me. I had lied and told her I was 18. I remember looking at what time it was and thought to myself.

"I thought she needed to get cigarettes from her car."
"Didn't you need to get something from your car?" I asked her.
"Oh yes!" She said. "Let's go."

We walked for a minute, ending up on another side of the apartment complex and came up to a white SUV. She opened up the car and searched it for a minute.

"Where did I put them?" She asked herself.
"It's okay" I told her. "I have some if you're out."

She shut the passenger door behind her and I handed her a cigarette. She looked at me and smiled. However; I knew I was lit as fuck from drinking.

We stood in place by the car and finished smoking.
"Should we go check in on your friends?" I asked her.
"No. We don't need to-- they'll be fine." She said.
I smiled and bolstered a short laugh. "Oh, are you sure?"
"You have a very nice smile." She says to me.
I couldn't help but blush and smile a little bigger for the compliment.
"Well, I think you are extremely gorgeous." I tell her. "And I appreciate you walking around with…"
Emma smiled and pulled me by my belt loop on my jeans.
"WHOA," I thought to myself. "This is odd."
"Come here." She says lingering her neck forward.
I kiss her once, twice and… the tongue appeared the third time. She stopped and took a step back.
"I'm sorry." She says to me.

"It's okay." I say giggling.

She placed her hand onto the side of my face and began kissing me again. I decided to just go with it. My hands, already placed on her hips, slid into her back pocket. She had moved one onto my groin and began feeling up that area. I try to stay quiet but let out a moan.

"Oh, fuck." Comes out of my mouth.

She began sucking on my neck and slipped one of her hands through my jeans...

Her hand motions were impeccable. She knew exactly what she was doing. She stopped sucking on my neck and looked at me enjoying her touch.

"Does that feel good?" She whispered in my ear.

"Yes" I murmured and grabbed her ass.

"Someone is going to see us." I tell her.

I hear keys jingle and the SUV unlock.

"Get in." She tells me.

I hopped in the backseat of the vehicle. She followed right behind me and closed the door. Quickly we began kissing and she hoisted herself on top of me. She pulled away for a second and took her shirt off. I went for my belt and by that time it was too late. She undid my belt and put me in her mouth.

"FUCK." I said. Leaning my head back into the seat.

My jeans weren't fully removed and she had manipulated me to become hard through the zipper. I wasn't wearing any underwear.

As soon as she stopped she removed her jeans and shifted the thong she was wearing to the side and grabbed my penis. And placed me inside her.

"Ohhh God…"

Her head rested on my shoulder, I grabbed her with both hands on her ass, and pushed myself deeper inside her. She continued to suck on my neck and breathe in my ear. I leaned into the backseat and bounced her on me for a while. She began to become loud and I could hear my phone going off in my jeans.

"Cum inside me." She tells me.
I won't lie. It almost killed my erection. I honestly thought, "Okay, yes, she is crazy."
Continuing to kiss her and bounce her on top of me, I came….
Inside her.
We stopped for a second and we began to kiss each other again. All I thought was.
"Oh shit… what did I do?"
She laughed and slid off me. Semen everywhere. Gross.

I tucked myself back into my jeans and threw my head back in satisfaction. The windows were a little bit foggy and the inside of the vehicle felt warm.

"It's fucking hot in here," She said and cracked the door open.
I laughed as she pulled her jeans on. I reached for my phone and saw 3 missed calls from Tracy, and a few text messages asking where I was. She did the same. We stepped outside of the vehicle and remained intimate touching and kissing each other. After a while her friends approached from a distance.

"What are you two doing out here?" One girl asked.
"Just hanging out," I replied to her.

One of the girls had long black curly hair and light brown eyes. Her other friend was blonde and appeared overtly intoxicated, leaning on a pole where the SUV was parked.

"Daniel this is Marla, and **that** drunk ass is Shelby," Emma tells me.
"Nice to meet you." I say holding my hand out to Marla.
"I'll uh, meet Shelby some other time." I say watching her lean on a pole.

Emma and her friends got into the SUV and left, after I exchanged phone numbers with Emma. I began to walk back towards Richie's apartment to find Tracy. I walked in with the most dumbfounded face and saw that the party had begun to wind down.
Tracy and Richie stood in the kitchen with body language that displayed some sexual shame.

"Hey guys." I say to them with a shit grin on my face.
"There you are!" Tracy says hugging me. "Where the fuck have you been?"
"Tracy... I.. just... don't even." I struggle to put words out and swallow hard.
"Something happen?" Tracy asked.
"Yeah."
"What happened?"
"I just had sex in the parking lot in this girl's SUV," I tell her smiling.
"What the fuck?!"
"Yeah. I'll let you know what happened later," I tell her.

After everyone had left, Tracy and I sobered up a little and drank water for the rest of the evening. I remember driving home as the sun began to rise, its rays stretching across the horizon. I had told Tracy the whole story on the way back home that night. I had also mentioned I thought she was being raped or killed when I couldn't find her, which she found comical.

"I can handle myself," She tells me.

As soon as she dropped me off, I crawled into bed with the blue haze of sunlight beginning to leak through my blinds in my room. My cat meowing at my door to see me and a consistent buzzing from my cell phone.

It was Emma.

I didn't reply and thought everything through. I was more concerned about her being pregnant or giving me an STD. I planned to rest throughout the morning and would follow up with her when I woke up.

🐰 Bridget 🐰

Septomber quickly arrived, my birthday month and my favorite time of the year for weather. Emma kept in touch with me and we would meet rarely. We did not get into a relationship but felt we had an agreement to only have sex with each other. The more I got to know her, the more she and I were casual. It actually felt pretty good.

My quiet room is where I remained. I decided to stick with late nights. I didn't re-enroll in school and dropped out again. Allowing myself to be fall further behind in the academic world. I hadn't spoken with my mother or my father for a while now. I ate when they were sleeping and often left the house at night. Luke worked overnights at a burger joint so I wasn't able to see him much. Tracy had decided to take college classes and got her sleep schedule sorted out. I began to consider not just dropping out of school. But I had no motivation. Only desire now. I only wanted to have sex, relax, drink, and smoke.
My phone went off while I was playing a video game. I looked at the number and pick up.

"Luke, hey?"
"Bored man, are you able to get out?"
"Yeah, I think my parents are sleeping." I tell him.

I grabbed my mother's keys and ran down to the garage. I pulled the emergency lever on the garage and lift the door up myself. I jump in the car and switch it to neutral. Then, pushing the car down the driveway and jumping in the seat to rotate the wheel. Getting out again I push the car down the street and leave quietly.

If I had left with someone else that night I didn't feel my parents would care. However taking the car was a different story.

I had went through the driveway to harass Luke, knowing his voice would be the one to take my order.

"What can I get for you this evening?"
"A dick."
"Sir?"
"A dick with a side of balls."
"Fuck you, Daniel."

I pulled up to the front and parked the car, watching Luke come outside with a cigarette in his mouth.

"You that bored?" I ask him.
"Yeah, it's dead tonight."
"I can tell." I tell him looking around the parking lot.

Luke and I talked on a bench that was outside the restraint where people ate. After a few minutes a girl walked out asking Luke to get something for her that she was too short to reach.

"Luke, I need to pull some of the to-go boxes I'm too short!" She says.
"Alright, give me a second."
Luke ran inside and shortly came back out.
"Who was that?" I ask him.
"Vanessa, she works nights with me."

I didn't find her attractive, and only asked out of curiosity.

"You should see her friend though that comes by." Luke tells me.

And eventually later that night I did, I hung around and talked with Luke through most of his shift. A girl in a white sedan rolled through the driveway and hopped out of the car to speak with Vanessa. We all grouped with each other and talked a little bit. Vanessa's friend was blonde-haired, blue – eyed, and had freckles. She was cute, but not really my type. It did nothing for my penis, and my perverted thoughts couldn't really create a mental porno either.

We laughed about a few things being that America was place where you could get a double cheeseburger that was cheaper than purchasing a salad. Eventually, I got her name and number. Bridget.

I texted her for a week. Not really pressing for sex or becoming hopeful. Shit, I didn't even want that. She appeared as if she had her life together and knew where she was going to take her life. A college student and a high school student who graduated earlier than anticipated. I took her out on a few dates and it was only until the 2nd date when we finally made something happen.

I haven't kissed her yet, held her hand or anything. She had called me late at night and asked if I was doing anything.

"I'm at home, just on my computer." I tell her. "You can come by," I add.
"Give me a few minutes." She told me.

I waited for almost an hour, when she called again to let me know that she was in front of my house. I walked downstairs and opened my front door. She wore a tight knitted sweater, brown leather boots that almost went to her knees, and those tight blue jeans I loved staring at.

"Come in." I tell her.

My house was dark, I had brought her up to my room, and turned on the television. I remember we began to spooning a little bit and her pushing her ass into my groin area. Feeling her moving her hips was a 'yes'. At least it's what it felt like.

I placed my hand on her thigh thinking she would grab my hand and hold it. Instead, she opened her leg a little bit more and rolled to her other side towards me. Looking straight at me without saying anything was obvious. We began kissing.

In a missionary position, I started to run my fingers on her clitoris. She lifted one leg up and removed one boot, then the other. I removed her jeans slowly, and began to kiss her neck, bit lightly on her ear, and worked myself down to her waist.

"Nothing smells." I kept the thought in my head. "Great."

I started to run my tongue not too light on her. And picked up the pace from there, keeping my tongue wide and loose as possible. After a few minutes her legs squeezed my head I felt like it was going to pop. Her legs began to shake, and he pulled me over to her and began undoing my belt. She leans up and puts her hands on my ass. Pushing myself inside her.

Personally feeling extra arousal from a missionary position was drab. It wasn't a way I could really enjoy myself but of course I wanted her to enjoy herself. Our movements were slow, and breathing was heavy. But what she did in the middle of it was so odd to me. She grabbed me by my ass again pushing myself deep inside her. One of her fingers pressed on my asshole.

"Harder." She whispered in my ear and nipped at it.

I tried to void out the feeling of getting my asshole pushed on. And kept sucking on her neck and kissing her. I pulled out and came on my bed.

We laid there for a second catching our breath. She didn't throw on her underwear and rested her head on my shoulder.

"I really like you." She says to me.
"I like you too." I told her back. "I'm going to get some water, you want some?"
"That's fine," She replies, nuzzling her face into one of my pillows.

I ran downstairs and saw my phone sitting on the kitchen counter, I pour two glasses of water and see a message notification on my phone. I put the glasses down and look into my phone. I opened it up.

"I'll be in your neighborhood. Would like to see you."
"Hey are you still up?"
Emma…

I didn't want to tell Bridget, or let Emma know what was going on. I don't think Emma would've cared but I enjoyed her company and Bridget's as well. I had already decided that a relationship at my age was foolish. I felt any relationship would last only a while then end up in flames.

I walked upstairs to my room and saw Bridget watching T.V and looking up at me as I walked in.

"Here you go." I tell her handing her water.
I decide not to text back Emma or bring it up with Bridget. A few minutes later, my phone being in my pocket now starts ringing.

"Oh shit." I told myself.

Bridget looked at me and asked "Who is calling you this late?"

"Must be one of my friends." I tell her.

I pull out my phone hoping it didn't read 'Emma'.

It was Luke.

"Hey man what's going on?" I ask him.

"Can I come over? My stepdad is being a dick right now."

"Yeah is everything okay?" I ask him.

"Yeah, I just can't be here right now." He tells me.

I hang up the phone and Bridget moves her head closer to my chin.

"Is he okay?"

"I don't know." I tell her.

"He sounded really upset." She says.

"Yeah, I'm going to go downstairs and wait for him."

"OK, I'm going to relax if that's okay?" She asked me.

"Of course."

I took my phone with me and threw a jacket on and waited for Luke to pull up. I sat on my driveway for a few minutes until I saw his familiar headlights pull into my neighborhood. Luke quickly parked, turned his car off, and jumped out.

"Fuck man. He is such a dick."

"What happened?" I asked holding out my arms squinting.

"Got into a fight with him, and he started throwing shit everywhere in the house." Luke says leaning on his car.

"You can sleep on the couch." I tell him. "Is your mom okay?" I ask.

"She's fine, she's staying in a hotel tonight until he calms down."

I have Luke follow me inside my house and let him know that Bridget was in my room. Something he wasn't surprised about.

"I'm going to check on her." I tell him.

I walk back upstairs and check on Bridget. She appeared sleeping and looked up at me.

"Is he okay?"
"Yeah, I'm going to talk to him for a bit." I tell her. "I just wanted to see if you're okay too." I add.
"I'm going to sleep a bit." She tells me.
"Okay. I'll be back."

I went downstairs to inquire more about his situation. Only to find that his stepdad was drinking and becoming belligerent to the point he couldn't stand to be in the house.

"Emma messaged me tonight."
"Okay, and?" Luke asked, laying down on the couch.
"She wants to see me tonight." I tell him.
"Oh shit you have Bridget here?"
"Yeah, she wants to come here too." I tell him.
"Just stay outside and talk to her." He tells me.
"That's a bad idea man."
"Well either way you are probably going to get caught." He tells me laughing.
"I'll talk to her."

I messaged back Emma, and within a few minutes received a call back. I could not ignore it.

"Hey, I'm by your place," She tells me.

I explained everything with Luke and didn't attempt to bring up Bridget. I don't know what I was doing. I told her she could drop by for a few minutes but I couldn't let her inside.

"I'll tell her this needs to stop." I told myself.

She pulled up to my house next to Bridget's car and Luke's. She didn't ask what the other cars were doing parked next to the driveway. She jumped out of her car and threw her arms around me and kissed me. I fucked up by letting her do so.

"How have you been?" She asked me pulling a cigarette out. "How is your friend?" She asked.
"He's okay." I tell her. "He is sleeping and had a rough night with his parents."
"Ah Okay." She says.
I spoke with her for a bit and asked what she was doing on my side of town.
"Marla moved nearby here." She tells me. "I'm probably going to move with her."
"Oh nice."

After she finished smoking I leaned on her vehicle, just hoping she would leave soon or say something. I could've easily just told her to go. However, she lived on the other side of town and I didn't want to force her out.

She put her hands on my sides and leaned on me. I kept looking at her and my front door knowing Bridget could walk out at any second. She kissed me on my lips and kissed multiple times on my neck. It felt good. I felt so wanted by her.

"We can't have sex." She tells me.

"That's fine." I say smiling. "I wasn't expecting anything." I tell her.

"I'm on my period." She adds.

After she had told me that, I felt relieved. Knowing that she wasn't pregnant.

"It's okay." I say giggling.

I grew paranoid that Bridget could walk out at any second.

"Hey can I see this SUV?" I ask her.

"You've seen inside of it." She said smiling.

"I wasn't paying that much attention to the vehicle." I tell her.

"Jump in." She says nudging her neck for me to get into the driver's side.

I place my hands on the steering wheel, and ask her about all the buttons on the dashboard. I look back and quickly gather mental images of her and I having sex in the backseat. She lifts up the center console in the vehicle which appeared to allow a third person to sit up front. She moves closer to me and places her head on my shoulder. She makes a kissing noise.

"Kiss me." She says.

I smile and do it anyway.

She started to kiss the side of my neck. I had a weakness for it. I looked at what time it was, and began to sink into the seat. She moved up to my ear and whispered.

"Pull the seat down."

I reached my hand to the side of the seat and leaned on it. She began to kiss my stomach and undid my belt.

"Off." She said, pulling on my jeans.

I arched my back and pulled my jeans down to my ankles. She starting sucking on me, moving her hand up my chest and around my waist. I loved looking at her lovely eyes while she went down on me.

"Oh my God." I say exhaling.
"Mhmm," she murmured.

It wasn't long until I came in her mouth. She held it in and opened the door and spit it out.

"I don't swallow." She starts to laugh.
"That's okay." I say giggling.
"Feel good?" She says placing her head on my shoulder again.
"Yes, very." I tell her. "I appreciate that."
"Mm good." She says pulling my hand and kissing it.

We laid there for about an hour. She mentioned she was growing tired and should probably head home. I kissed Emma goodbye as she slid over to the driver's seat and drove off. I stood in my driveway until she was gone from sight. I walked to my front door and stopped. I placed my hand on my forehead and leaned on the wall next to my front door. I slid down it slowly and brought my knees to my chest. I felt horrible emotionally, even though I was physically satisfied.

"I'm a fucking dipshit." I tell myself.
I gather myself emotionally, and walk back into the house. I walk over to the couch and find Luke laying down watching T.V.
"How'd it go?"
"Dude. I feel kind of shitty."
"What happened?" Luke sat up.

I explained what Emma and I just did and was not proud of it at all.

"Oh fuck. Did you sleep with Bridget?"

"Yes, just before all of that." I say.

"It felt nice at the time, now I don't even know." I tell him sitting on the couch and rubbing my eyes.

"What are you going to do?"

"No idea, I'm surprised my dick didn't smell like another girl's vagina." I say.

"She couldn't tell?"

"Doesn't matter does it?" I reply.

I sulked on the couch, feeling guilty. I didn't want to go back upstairs.

"This is your shit." Luke tells me.

I don't reply to Luke and stand up. I leave the room telling him, "I'll figure it out."

I went into the bathroom and quickly showered. Grabbing a towel I went into my room and decided to act as normal as possible. Bridget was sound asleep…

I got clothes from my drawer and threw on some shorts and shirt. I crawled into bed with her. She woke up briefly and began to pick at her eye.

"Is everything okay?" She asked me

"Yeah Luke passed out on the couch downstairs."

"Good." She said to me while resting her head on my shoulder.

"Do you have class tomorrow?" I asked her.

"No, I don't have anything planned."

"That's good." I say.

I felt her hands run down my shorts. I grab her on the wrist gently and continue to stare at the T.V.

"I'm tired." I tell her.

She kissed me on my shoulder and retracted her arm.

"Okay."

She rolled over to her side as I continued to watch T.V. Guilt is what I felt. Disgusting, and remorseful for my actions. I did however, like the attention and physical attraction I felt from Emma and Bridget.

My phone was kept downstairs now, I watched useless television shows until I eventually passed out. I woke up the next morning to Bridget sucking on me. I couldn't resist.

She left early, and I went downstairs to check on Luke. He was passed out on the couch. I sat on the couch with a cup of coffee and waited for him to wake up. I turned the television on and kept the volume low. After an hour Luke woke up.

"I'm going to break it off with both of them." I tell him.
"Sounds like a good idea." He says.

I couldn't think of words that describe how I felt. And you by now would agree what I did was garbage.
It changed for me from there.

Recollection

Bridget and I quickly broke it off. I had called her two days shortly after telling her I wasn't ready for a relationship and that we should stop all communication. She was mad, upset, and called me a few nasty things. I didn't fire back at her, hell why would I? I deserved everything she told me. The only words that weren't spoken were "You're a liar." I had attempted to talk to Emma in person and sent her multiple messages so I could speak with her in person. However, it never seemed like she was interested in a relationship. I was just a penis to her.

I spoke with Luke again about the issue, stating that I would not be seeing any girls or had a desire to go looking. Instead, I placed my time back into school and focused on what was important.

I hadn't spoken to my mom or my dad in quite a while. During dinner, I would take my plate and walk it upstairs to my room avoiding my parents. Afterwards I would walk downstairs and place the plate next to the dishwasher and blankly tell my mom, "Thank you."

If my dad ever tried to speak with me, I would ignore him and go into my room without saying a word. I could see that my mom was always worried during those nights. I decided eventually I would try to speak with them again about some emotional problems. Just not now.

I spoke with Tracy and Luke on most nights studying school work and had reached a point where I hadn't been drinking. My dad caught on to the missing booze and I thought it would be great if I was alone for a while concentrating on myself. Instead many women passed through my periphery and many late nights with pornographic sites became routine. I decided to explore pornography a little bit more.

Gangbangs, cream-pies, bukkake, lesbian, hentai, bestiality, bondage, strip-tease, foot fetishes, vintage, face-fucking and role playing. Yep, I have seen it all. And believe me when I say that is just a quarter of the list of things I have actually looked into. Some videos were alien to me, but I still found pleasure in watching them. I didn't desire any emotional attachment at this point because I had porn, friends, and my solitude. I felt golden.

A few months went by and I had dropped out of school again. This time I went on the normal habits of meeting up with Tracy and Luke at that mall parking lot late at night. Going on about drinking and ranting about parents, and finding something else to do with our time. That night in the parking lot Tracy had shown a picture to me on her phone.

"Who is this?" I ask her.
"Tyler." She tells me.
I look at her phone and see a tall white guy, who appeared taller than Tracy.
"Okay?" I say and hand her back the phone.
"I'm thinking about dating him." She says
"Well I hope it works out for you." I tell her.

I wasn't really interested in her love life. Seeing how things ended up with her last boyfriend. She never did talk to him again after that night that I had met Emma. But of course I would check in on her to see if she would establish a relationship. Luke had met a girl outside of a sushi restaurant and began dating. He kept in touch, but spent most of his free time with her.

As more months went by, I had enrolled back into school and completed my high school diploma. My father was the happiest that I had ever seen him and my mother looked a little bit more cheerful. Happy that I wasn't a complete failure from what it felt like. I graduated with my original class even though none of those classmates realized it. I didn't walk at graduation and instead drank on my driveway that night thinking that my life should be as it was.

Still, with no direction, I continued late nights and made no plans where to go from there. Playing computer games until Tracy or Luke decided to get ahold of me. One night Tracy finally did. And it had been awhile since I had seen her. My dad was happy I completed high school and had bought a cheap Honda that I used to get around. I was extremely appreciative of it but wished he and I could be friends. Buying a car for me, supporting a roof over my head, and even paying for my cell phone at this time had made me greatly appreciate him. But It didn't feel like I had someone to talk to. Someone who was my family who showed care in other ways. To be emotional for once, and level with me about my personal problems.

Tracy had given me an address that night. I drove over into a neighborhood that I had never been to before. It was extremely nice and appeared that you had to have money to live in the community. All the houses were white, driveways were big and had three to four car garages. As soon as I arrived Tracy was on the driveway with who appeared to be Tyler.

"Hey what's going on?" I say getting out of my car.
"Hello Daniel." Tracy says hugging me. "There is someone I'd like you to meet."
"Okay." I say.
"Hey man, Tyler." He says holding his hand out.

"Nice to meet you. Finally." I tell him.

He was taller than Tracy, and had a deep voice. Light skin and blonde hair. He was at least 6'3". Compared to Tracy's 6'0" and my 5'9". I felt like I was surrounded by Xena the princess warrior and the green bean giant. I guess some fairytales do appear to end happily ever after. Tracy and Tyler and I would drink and hang out. The house he lived in was enormous and appeared to live there by himself.

"How do you afford this man?" I ask
"My dad is a doctor, it's only me though."
"So where does he live?" I ask.
"In New Mexico. But I'm here for now."

I looked around to what was mostly a big empty house. Tyler and I became pretty close friends and we shared a few stories about growing up. We became close friends rather quickly. Tracy started to deteriorate her feelings towards Tyler and focus on other boys as soon as she felt bored with him. Another night Tracy had called me.

"Daniel."
"Offices of Daniel, how can I help you today?"
"No, this is serious." She says with a low voice.
"Fine, what's going on?"
"I took Tyler's virginity."
"OH DAMN." I say with my mouth open over the phone.
"Then I broke up with him." Tracy tells me.
"What? Tracy what? Why?" I stutter.
"I'm just not that into him I guess." She tells me and starts laughing.
"Were you at least nice?" I ask.
"I don't know, just told him and I don't really care." She tells me.

I could only imagine how Tyler was feeling. Fuck, that wasn't cool at all. Tracy was my friend but I figured she would at least be in a deeper commitment with him than that. Feelings for Jen flooded back, and I remembered how I'd felt when she decided to be a bitch to me and forget me, how broken and empty I was. Like I was nothing. I knew Tyler felt that he was nothing. And he couldn't understand why.

I didn't have his number that night. As soon as Tracy and I got off the phone I decided to get in my car and drive over. I knocked on his door and heard some music playing in the background. Tyler answered the door and appeared to have some redness in his eyes.

He knew I knew.

"You alright?" I ask him.

That night I had talked to Tyler, and told him I didn't approve of Tracy's way. However she was always going to be my friend. Tyler explained to me what happened and did not understand what went wrong. He felt remorseful, confused, and showed a little bit of anger with each detail. I cannot remember much of that conversation, but I do remember how bad she hurt him.

"I'm both your friends." I tell him. "I'll stick with both of you regardless of good decisions or bad ones." I add.

Tyler was thankful, I got his number and we developed a closer relationship. A bond like brothers.

A few days went on. I had picked up a job working for a cell phone company and managed my time during the day and at night. My sleep schedule was normal, and I always had money in my pocket. Life was good. The few friends I had were nice, I created a porn playlist off a website, and would have a nightly routine. Watch porn, message friends, shower, and sleep. The next day would start off with work and I would look forward to the weekends. Fuck, my life felt squared away. Tyler had called that weekend for myself to come over. A few other of his friends were there with a few beers and it was nice getting away from that parking lot that I had always met Tracy and Luke in.

"Daniel. Look at this." Tyler hands me his phone.
The picture showed a positive pregnancy test.
"Tyler? Dude… you ok?"
Tyler started to breathe heavily and dropped his phone on the floor.
"There's no way." I said to myself out loud.
"No there fucking isn't," Tyler added.

Tyler grabbed his phone and began searching images online. After an hour he found the exact same image of a positive pregnancy test. The same image that Tracy had sent him.

"That bitch." Tyler says.

Tyler and I laughed a bit as he sighed in relief. I was a little disappointed in Tracy's actions and called her later that night as I drove home.

"Seriously, Tracy." I tell her.
"What?"
"A picture you found online?" I ask.
Tracy began to laugh. "Okay, I'm a bitch."
"I just don't get why you would do that." I tell her.
"To be a bitch," she says.
"Alright I'll talk to you later." I say to her and hang up.

As soon as I pull up to my house I look at my phone and see that Tracy has messaged me.

"Are you mad?"
It read.

I ignored her message and went on with my nightly routine. The next day Tracy showed up to my house to talk to me.

"You're mad at me?" She asked.
"No" I tell her crossing my arms. "You hurt him once." I say.
"You care?" She asks me.
"He's my friend Tracy." I tell her. "You are too."

Tracy apologized to Tyler. I had advised them both not to talk to each other. Tracy also seemed a little jealous of my relationship with Tyler. The more and more Tyler and I began to hang out, the less I saw of Tracy.

There were many nights at Tyler's. I didn't hear much from Luke or Tracy. I made new acquaintances and created many memories hanging out with Tyler. He was an exact opposite of Tracy and Luke, not in a bad way, either. Had goals with his life directly after high school, and had a great family. He was generous and kind and always appeared honest and open with me.

As my work schedule continued, I decided to enroll in a community college and start taking a few classes. Tracy and I ended up enrolling around the same time and reconnected. Luke had been around messaging me a bit letting me know that his relationship had ended. I empathized with him and thought to myself that I hadn't been with a girl in a long time.

And that wasn't going to change. I didn't want it to. Tyler gave me a call close to the upcoming weekend. I was browsing through the mall and ran into a familiar face.

"Hey…" A voice close to me says.
I turn around and see a snake wrapped around this guy's neck. Baggy black jeans, and long hair.
"Yeah you were in my…uh…" I start snapping my fingers.
"Interior design class." He says.
"YES. Lots of girls." I tell him smiling.
"That's the only reason I took it." He says to me.
We both laugh.
"Thomas." He tells me.

I talk to him a bit and grab his number. Thinking it was nice to see a familiar and nice face. I drove over to Tyler's before the day was over, shortly after leaving the mall. I get out of my car, and see a girl with blonde hair and ignore her completely. I turn to Tyler, smiling.

"Dude I just ran into a guy I haven't seen in a while." I tell him smiling.
"Oh nice. How was tha-" Tyler cuts off.
"You have really nice teeth." The blonde headed girl says to me.
Tyler and I both look at her. He starts to laugh.
"Daniel this is my friend Andrea."
I place my hands in my pockets, and lift my chin up.
"Nice to meet you." I tell her.

I let Tyler know of the old friend I ran into and left shortly. I didn't have a desire to know who Andrea was nor really cared. My week went on normally. Tyler invited me over his house that weekend to a party he was hosting at his place. I figured why the fuck not? It's been awhile since I drank and I haven't gotten out much.

Girls I've never seen before, a few guys whom I have, and of course no surprise, Andrea was there as well. I only talked to Tyler, and didn't really try to talk to any of the girls. A few of the guys were nice, always seemed to ensure I had a beer in my hand and took a few shots with them. I could make out in the corner of my eye Andrea looking at me. Sometimes I could catch her through a reflection in the window. I ignored everything.

"Nope, fuck that." I told myself.

Later that night I walked up to Tyler's room with him.

"Have you talked to Tracy at all?" He asks me.

"Nah man why?" I ask back.

"Cause she's a bitch." He tells me laughing.

"Sometimes we talk."

"Oh God." He says.

I finish my beer, and run through images in my head of Andrea looking at me when I'm turned around.

"I like how your blonde friend likes my teeth." I tell him laughing.

"She's a nice girl. You interested?" He asks me.

"Dude, fuck no." I tell him. "She looks like she's about to fall over any minute and start throwing up." I add.

"Wouldn't be the first time." He tells me.

Tyler and I walked onto a balcony in his house.

"I'm still kind of butthurt of how Tracy treated me." He tells me.

"I don't blame you."

"I wish you knew how I felt." He tells me.

"I can guess." I say to him.

I told Tyler about Jen. And a few of the previous girls. I sympathized with Tyler until we heard a knock on his bedroom door.

"Hold on a second." Tyler says walking towards the door.

Andrea stumbles in.

"Why is the door locked?" Andrea says looking at Tyler.

I began to walk back downstairs past Andrea and Tyler. I turn to Tyler. "We can finish this conversation later." I tell him.

I look at Andrea and smile. "Were having **GAY** sex Andrea." I say to her sarcastically. I close the door behind me and say out loud. "Fucking retard."

A few minutes later, Tyler and Andrea both appeared downstairs.

"What's up?" I look at Tyler.

"Eh, she just wanted to talk."

"Cool." I tell him.

As the night winded down, a few of the girls slept together in the same room. I stayed with Tyler in his room and slept on his floor. Things felt perfect. I had a friend who I could tell a few stories to. And I could relate with someone who appeared to genuinely listen to my emotions. I didn't forget about Thomas, I would get to him sometime. As my work weeks ran through I spent time with Tyler, and school. There were multiple times he invited me over to his place to drink and hang out. After a few more nights, Andrea made a few appearances and it was obvious she had an interest in me. Even if I had been a complete asshole to her.

There were times Tyler would talk to me and ask if I was interested in her. And there were multiple times he reiterated to her that I wasn't interested. However, after a few drunken evenings spent at his house, I had made the mistake. Being mildly flirtatious with Andrea, playing beer pong with her. I figured fuck since I've been such an asshole and she doesn't care then I figured she would be pretty cool. And she was, eventually I viewed her as a friend. Seeing so much of her at Tyler's house I couldn't continue to be an asshole all the time. She thought it was funny and never took it personally. She beat me with kindness. Damnit…

Andrea, had me. That night I felt the weather of fall, the soft breeze flowing through the air on Tyler's balcony. Sneaking off somewhere in Tyler's house with Andrea and kissing. That same night as everyone was leaving, Tyler knew what was going on and just smiled about the whole thing. Andrea and I went into a guest room, locked the door and turned off the lights. She began kissing me as I reached up her dress and felt her breasts. I rolled over and placed myself on top of her and positioned her legs around my waist. My hand on her face and lightly a brush through her hair with my fingers. I kiss her on the neck and suck on it. Kissing her again there, then, her collar. I move towards her breasts, stomach, and then her waist. Moving under the covers of the bed.

"Thank God! No smell." I think to myself.

She allows me to take my time. And like always, I let my tongue loose and allow her to get used to my movement. I finger her at the same time, spit on her clit, and lightly suck on it. I feel her hand control my head and where she wants me to go. I allow it. Her thighs tighten a bit. I move up towards her and start to kiss her neck. She grabs my hard cock and directs it into her, I push eagerly, and felt maybe it was too quick.

"Shi…" She lets out.

Her mouth opened and froze for a second. I kept one arm wrapped around her and the other on the side of her cheek with my thumb and pointer finger cupped by her ear.

There was no protection, which was of course, stupid. I felt her hands on my back, and her nails lightly dig in my skin. Her hand moved down to my ass and pushed me forward. I pulled out, and came on the mattress. (Sorry Ty.)

The rest of the night, I remember staring at each other. I can't remember a damn thing I was thinking. But I knew I told myself.

"I'll give this a shot."

🐰 Andrea 🐰

Winter's cold grip was back. Andrea and I moved pretty quickly. Things were swell at first. But it appeared that we started to destroy each other rather than help each other grow. It wasn't easy for me to get into a relationship. As a matter of fact, my thoughts were that if a relationship ended, the pain would always be there. Memories that you held onto and questions asking myself if my life had been different if I had spent time with other people. However, giving Andrea a shot at a relationship was a tough one for me emotionally and I followed her at her pace.

She was supportive of my job, and even brought me lunch on some days. But there were issues that seemed to arise quickly. As soon as I became emotional or decided to talk to her about any issues that came to mind, she would laugh them off and disregard them completely. I ignored this for a while and thought maybe I was being a baby. But when Andrea had issues or something that was bothering her, I was expected to listen and be attentive to her problems. I had no issue about it but it wasn't reciprocated. Sex was normal, and we did not have a dull moment when it came to that. Until, of course, a pregnancy scare hit the table.

"We need to talk." She tells me over the phone.
"Alright." I reply. "Is everything okay?" I asked.
"I'll tell you later." She says to me.

I drove over to her house. Her face was drab, uninterested in anything, and depression was felt throughout her body language.

"What's going on?" I asked her.

She hid a pregnancy test under her bed, and pulled it out. Showing a positive sign. At first, I thought of what Tracy did to Tyler. I didn't bring that up in this case. My trust for her was lessened. I couldn't understand how she could be pregnant especially since the time she told me didn't match with the last time we had even been intimate. She was focused on school and I was focused on work. Something didn't add up. But I supported her anyway.

"What do you want to do?" I asked her.
"I am not having a child." She tells me. "No fucking way." She adds.
"Alright." I tell her. "Whatever you decide, I'll help you."

She had asked to be left alone the rest of the evening. I spoke with one of her friends, whom was more my friend through an acquaintance at the mall I used to go to. She was more than willing to talk about the issues I had wanted to utter.

Her house was nice, her parents were welcoming. They didn't even know me and were extremely sweet. Janelle was her name. Long dark hair and brown eyes. Slim body type and very cute. I had a crush on her at a time but like Tracy, she had an interest in one guy after the next.

"Andrea told me she was pregnant." I look down on my lap. "Saw the test." I added.
"Seriously?" She said with her eyes widening. "Are you going to keep it?"

We sat in her backyard, on a table. She started to twirl her hair in thought, her eyes would cross over the patio ceiling.

"Hmm. What do you want?" She asked me.

"I'm not one for abortions." I tell her. "But it's not **only** my choice."

It was nice to have someone listen and care. I could've talked to Tyler, however, he had been out of town visiting his parents in New Mexico. Janelle was around for Tyler's parties and we would casually say hello to each other.

"I had an issue too." She tells me and places her hands together.

"What's that?" I ask.

Janelle mentioned a name of a boy I knew. Whom she had caught chlamydia from. It didn't sound as bad, I mean, it's treatable. But of course catching it from someone you slept with without any knowledge must have sucked. I left Janelle's home, and called Andrea asking if I could swing by. Janelle and I promised each other to keep our secrets to ourselves, and never mention it again.

As soon as I got to Andrea's she had told me to walk in. I greeted her mother and saw Andrea lying on her bed in the dark.

"Okay, maybe she isn't full of shit." I thought to myself.

I laid next to her and began to brush my fingers through her hair.

"You okay?" I asked her.

Andrea sighed and wrapped her arms around me.

"You need anything?" I asked.

Andrea shook her head.

I left the house later that night and got in touch with Thomas. He was up late, and I thought we could get together. As soon as I met up with him, I told him the story of Andrea. He was very likeable, calm and understanding. I wondered why we weren't friends earlier.

A few weeks went by, and there was no sign of Andrea being pregnant. Which kind of thwarted my thoughts of her actually being honest with me. Later one afternoon she had called me.

"There is something I need to tell you." She says over the phone.
"Okay, what's going on?" I ask.

We met up later that evening and she had told me that she had taken a pill that caused a miscarriage. She appeared physically drained and pained. I asked myself questions and thought why she wouldn't talk to me about this when it happened.

My trust deteriorated as I didn't believe it to be true. But I continued to listen to her and support her decision. As a few more days went by Andrea had angrily drove to my house and started getting in my face on the driveway.

"Did you tell, Janelle?" She asked pointing her finger at me.
"I did tell her." I say.

Andrea turned away and got back into her car and drove off. I immediately messaged Janelle.

"Dude what the fuck." I say to her.
"What?"
"Who did you go around telling?" I ask her.
"Nobody." She says to me.

I hung up the phone and stayed in my room the rest of that night. I hoped Andrea would calm down. Instead, I forwarded the messages that I received from Janelle to Andrea. Showing her that she was the only person that I had talked to. Of course I lied because I had told Thomas as well.

Sooner or later, Andrea had to calm down. She did, however our relationship was distant. We spent less time together, and she started to preoccupy her weekends without letting me know until the last second. I couldn't help but feel hurt. For a month she started to make plans with friends and appeared to never have time for me. I went along with it, though.

I decided she maybe just needed time to be around others who cared about her. Tyler and Thomas and I spent time together over those weekends. Until of course I received a call from Andrea.

"What are you up to?" She asked. She also sounded a little intoxicated.
"I'm with Tyler and Thomas right now." I told her.
Since I had made plans with them, I decided to say there and stick with what I promised. Andrea didn't like that very much.
"Okay, fuck you too." She tells me.
As soon as she hung up, I looked at my phone and said out loud to myself,"What the fuck."
I looked quickly to Tyler and Thomas.
"What the fuck is her problem lately?" I look at them.
"Maybe she's on her period?" Thomas says laughing.
"Seriously guys." I tell them.
Tyler starts to cover his mouth.
"Okay,that wasn't nice, maybe she just wants to see you." Tyler tells me.
"Yeah, but she hasn't made any plans with me in almost a month now." I tell them.

Andrea has been going out to parties over the weekends. I refuted to succumb to her instant requests. I sent her a text message and waited a response which I didn't receive that night.

I wasn't going to be on standby all the time and wait for her to want to see me. Shit got old quick, and eventually we made immense of the situation and started to spend time together. However, she would go back and forth without speaking with me for weeks and then demanding last minute that I should be with her or see her on a limb. Eventually pissed off and tired of the bullshit, I felt that there was more going on than just a lack of communication. On a cold night I decided to head over to a party and see a few friends with Thomas. Andrea walked right past me in the same complex. As if I were a complete stranger.

I felt hurt and confused. My heart rate picked up a bit. She had looked right at me. I went to my friend's apartment and could see the other apartment from his balcony.

"Do you know who lives there?" I asked the owner of the place.
"Yeah, I know him." He told me.

With a beer in my hand, I attempted to sort out my emotions and make sense of everything I was feeling. The name the man told me was a familiar name. One that I had actually had memories with in my elementary years.

I stayed outside the balcony that night with Thomas. I didn't see Andrea leave but figured it was late and that she might've left by now. I went down to the apartment and met a man with his hat backwards, glasses, skinny jeans, and curly brown hair.

"Dylan." I look at him smiling. "Remember me?" I ask.

"Of course I do." He tells me hold his hand out. "How have you been?"
He asked.

He invited me inside his place. I sat down and talked to him for a
second only to find out that Andrea had been fucking him as well.
I wanted to scream and punch him in the face.

I didn't, though. I stayed calm and talked to him about everything. He
let me know what was going on and it actually turned out that he had
a girlfriend as well. But you know that saying "Bros before Hoes" was
something he believed in. I thought commitment without lying
would've been a better terminology to go by.

I thanked him for his time. He gave me his number and I went on my
way back to see Thomas. I had told him everything in tears, with my
eyes red and my face becoming blank. I had devoted my emotions into
one girl and felt the worst pain in my chest.

Thomas drove me home that night. I didn't say anything else. There
were more issues with Andrea-- I felt entitled to know why she had
done what she did, however she never spoke with me. I gave up hope
talking to her and even then I wanted to resolve things peacefully. She
didn't seem to care, though; once a cheater always a cheater. And I
could never forgive her.

Andrea was my second girlfriend, and it took a lot of bravery to trust
her. I never wanted to be in a relationship in the first place and I didn't
want to invest time in someone who wouldn't respect my efforts to be
with them. Days turned into months, dreading what Andrea did to me.
I told Tracy who seemed to be more sympathetic and became
infuriated. Luke, who had met her at a point in our relationship,

expressed his hatred for her from the second she met her. It was going to take time to recover emotionally, but in the end it was for the best. To not be with a person who appeared to be malicious and un-caring for others' emotions. I saw her as a monster or someone who was more insensitive than me at times. This desensitized me more towards relationships. I wouldn't take another risk.

🐰 <u>Maggie</u> 🐰

I had a flair for picking the wrong girls. Not that they're ever wrong at the time, but I wonder what drew me to her. Maggie.

She was completely Aryan – blonde hair, blue eyes – the whole shebang. And boy, did she bang. Not that I'm complaining, either, because she was pretty sexy, too.

It was freshman year in college, and I didn't think much of anything when a new girl chose to sit next to me in English. Despite not knowing each other, we started talking almost immediately. The teacher – who the hell can remember his name? – didn't say anything when she and I would exchange whispers about how stupid the books we were reading were – no one cared about the Secret Society of the Summer Session or whether Piggy lived or died. We laughed at his ass-mar quite a bit. Everyone did.

It was funny: we talked shit on all the books we were forced to read, talked shit about everyone in the class around us, but I didn't even know her name for a long while, and I'm pretty sure she didn't know mine. I went the entire first two weeks without learning what her name was, until out of nowhere she grabbed my hand, made an exaggerated shaking motion, simultaneously introducing herself. Said her name was Maggie, and she thought it was pretty fucking stupid we didn't know each other's names yet. I agreed.

I liked her name, but I doubt I ever told her. It would've been a stupid thing to say.

My first kiss with Maggie happened pretty quickly: we'd known each other only for a few weeks before she leaned in. I leaned in, too, and from there, things moved faster than a cheetah on speed.

Blowjobs, fucking, making out, and more fucking. That's all we did. Hell, I think she was hornier than me.

She had a thing for blowjobs. Man, did she have a real thing for blowjobs. It was like…every time a parent went into another room or the lights were off during a movie, she took the opportunity she saw. I filled her mouth every time, and she smiled after. She was like what winning the sex lottery must feel like – I was never unsatisfied.

It wasn't until the second month of fucking Maggie that I realized we weren't even in a relationship.

"Hey," I said, lying naked on top of her, "are you my girlfriend?"
She laughed, then gripped my ass and pulled me into her. I didn't get an answer until I finished.
"Would I be fucking some random guy this hard?"
"I have no idea who you'd be fucking," I said.
I didn't really like her laugh, but I'm glad she thought I was funny.
"It's only you, stupid."
But I didn't think I was stupid.

The only time I really minded Maggie's libido was when I was driving. I'd feel a hand sliding over my junk, up to my belt. She was really good at undoing my belts.

"What the hell are you doing?" I'd shout, hands clutching at the wheels harder than she'd clutch my dick.

Instead of answering, she pulled my zipper down and ripped my dick out. She wouldn't even look at me throughout this, like it was a prize she couldn't take her eyes off. It never ceased to amaze me how I was always hard even before she pulled my pants down.

Driving with my pants around my knees was pretty fricking difficult, and trying to focus on the road with her mouth on my cock was even harder. More than once, she'd just bend my arm over her so she could just start a blowjob. Every few seconds I'd glance down to see her bob,

bob, bobbing, and I prayed we didn't pass any cops. I'm sure they'd pick up on what we're doing better than anyone else. Fortunately for us, we never passed any.

After a few months of dating and probably two dozen instances of this happening, I got used to it. Blowjobs and road head were just a thing with her, I guess – a fetish, if something so common can be called a fetish.

A few weeks or months later, she started to get bored of giving me head every five minutes. Or she had a lust for variety like me that made her agree to my request. I'd wanted to do it for a while, but she'd always been hesitant.

"Are you sure?" I'd asked.
"If you don't put it in yourself, I'll put it in for you," she said. I smirked, not needing any more of an invitation. She'd already lubed it up with her mouth, so I just shoved it right in…her ass. It felt great, and I loved hearing her moan. I finished almost as quickly as I did when putting it in her pussy, and she begged for more as soon as I came.

I almost felt bad that I couldn't give her any more.

"How often do you masturbate?" The question was off-putting by itself, but it came out of nowhere, and I think that's why I got so defensive.

"I dunno, maybe twice a week?" I guessed. I had no fucking clue how often I touched myself.

"Why the fuck…" she said, not finishing her thought. She was clearly irritated. I worried she was going to have a bald spot soon, from how she was plucking at her hair. When she was really angry, she'd start pulling at it, and I saw several small chunks come out. It was sad, because it was pretty hair.

"What?" I said, not really wanting to hear the answer. I knew this was going to be bad, no matter what direction she took it.

"You shouldn't be touching yourself," she said. "Not when you have me."

Her arms crossed her chest, pressing her pert tits out of her shirt a little. I wished my cock wasn't aware of this. Worse, I couldn't take my eyes off of them, because the glare on her face would terrify me.

"You're not always there," I shrug. Maybe she didn't hear the slight quiver in my voice.

"Fuck you," she shouts. She stood from the couch – as I'd heard her parents call it, the "loveseat" – and kept pressing her tits up, arm bent to pull on her hair, of course.

I remember thinking it was a stupid argument, but whatever made me say it...well, I wish I hadn't told her I thought it was stupid, that I couldn't masturbate. I wonder what she'd have thought if she knew I looked at porn sometimes, too. Probably would've punched me in the teeth.

At some point in the argument, I decided I had to stop worrying about making Maggie angrier, because everything made Maggie angrier.

I'd been dating Maggie for five months when I realized I hadn't seen any of my friends in five months.

I mean, I'd definitely *seen* them, I just never really interacted with them. Just the few minutes at school between classes, that's all. I was always with Maggie, fucking her, I mean, and that meant I couldn't hang with them. I really wanted to, but she hated them.

Even when I did see them, I couldn't be honest.
"Hey, what's up?" I'd been asked any number of times, just in passing through the hall.

"Oh, you know," I'd start, then weigh my options. "Just fucking my beautiful girlfriend all the time. That's about it."

Then we'd laugh, because we were kids. I didn't want to laugh, not really, but it would be weird if I didn't. I doubt anyone I talked to knew I missed them, that I wasn't even able to see them. It was just one of *those* relationships, I guess.

 "What the fuck is this?" I asked, holding a spent condom.
She shrugged.

It was hard, letting the shit hit the fan from the aphorism. I liked Maggie, despite her weird obsession with giving me blowjobs, her slightly controlling nature. After all, I'd been fucking her for almost six months, and we were close. It might be cliché to say, but I knew everything about her: why she thinks KFC is a stupid name (even though it's not), how she goes to the bathroom (she flushes while still on the toilet, for some reason)…*every*thing.

And the fact of the matter was, we *had* dated for just about six months, so I wasn't going to let it go that easily – that's a long time, after all.

I'd found the condom under her bed. It wasn't mine – I always used ribbed, but this one was just some run-of-the-mill shit. I was disappointed, not just because she was cheating on me, but also because I'd spent extra for the ribbing – I thought it mattered to her. Apparently all that mattered was the nonstop sex.

I repeated my question, about what the fuck that cum-filled condom was doing in her room, when it clearly was not mine, and she still didn't say anything. I kept prodding, for any answer, even if it was just to tell me she'd cheated on me. But she didn't say anything.

Well, she did tell me to get out.

From then on, things were strained between us. It wasn't that we didn't know there was a problem – we both knew exactly what was going on

– but she pretended like nothing was wrong. All she'd do was ignore me, treat me like shit when no one else was around...I just wanted her to apologize. She couldn't say she was sorry though, when she didn't feel guilty about what she'd done.

Maggie, my second girlfriend, cheated on me and didn't care.
Our relationship ended just a few days before our six-month anniversary.

I don't know what I learned from Maggie, if I learned anything at all. The end of our relationship was remarkably sad, and I don't really understand why she chose to cheat on me. So what it comes down to, I guess, is that she hurt me, and I stung for months after.

The girl I'd whisper with in English turned out to be a bitch, when all I wanted was for her to be a fun time. We didn't talk after we broke up. I didn't mind.

Marla and Tina

Maggie left my mind, and I strived to keep a distance with women. Of course I still had porn to watch if I ever felt lonely.

This doesn't sound so bad on the surface – what's a dry spell here and there? – but for me, it was almost normal.

I worked with some very difficult people at a restaurant. Some shitty café. The pay was mostly under the table, but I didn't mind – it bought me food and my clothes that weren't sold in malls. Sure, most boys can care less about clothes, but what else was I going to do? Wasn't a big deal then, not really one now.

My bedroom was plain and simple, clothes were organized in my closet by color and not a scent of a woman was present. As it was, all I had of my own was dark-colored shirts, a few pairs of pants, and an alarm clock. I had sold my T.V and computer to eventually upgrade later on. And I guess a single set of twin-sized sheets and toiletries. I bought food as I needed. Spartans had nothing on me, and it was pretty cool to say that I lived so modestly.

I think my employers suspected I was mostly poor, though. They asked why I was always wearing the same black shirt. Two of the half dozen shirts I had were black, so I can understand why it'd be weird showing up for three shifts a week in a black shirt and tight jeans. I always told them that too much variety might be too shocking. Dressing like a cartoon character, wearing the same clothes every day, wasn't so bad. Cartoon characters never die, at least.

One day, I walked in with a bit of a splurge – I was rushing in a few hours before my shift just walking around, and I decided to go to

Starbucks. Even bought a drink. A venti Americano, even got the biggest size.

I was thinking, as I walked into work, that I hadn't had real coffee since I was seeing Emma. She was kind of attractive, but really weird. I missed her, the way you might miss the last slice of pizza. Except, like the last slice of pizza, she was a bit much after the other seven slices.

Even so, I decided I'd pay her a visit. I knew she wouldn't mind. She had been going to college nearby, and I remembered she gave me an address. She wasn't terribly far from me, anyway. Or, she wasn't too far away for me to make a pass at her. Sure, it was a little sketchy, but I knew she'd love it.

I had trouble at work that day. Emma hadn't left my mind, and I kept messing up orders because of it. It was odd, because I had no idea why she was on my mind in the first place. Probably what happens when you let your dick do all the talking.

"Daniel, focus," said the old Italian man who owned the place. "You forgot table six's breadsticks."

"Sorry," I said, hardly listening to him. I grabbed the breadsticks and mumbled "Enjoy" before immediately turning back to the kitchen. I was yo-yoing my phone in and out of my pocket, trying to decide if I should text her or just surprise her. In the end, I decided it'd be a surprise – at least then, she couldn't just turn me down.

It was a long eight hours – even for that restaurant – but I finally made it out. I decided to drive over, despite the darkness. Or, darkness for my town, since there are always streetlights to deter the various criminals. Man, I fucking hated the place.

I found her building with no problem, but I had to wait for someone else to go in to make it past the security gate. It was getting a little late for a surprise rendezvous, but I wasn't worried about it. Emma was more of an insomniac than me – I think she took pride in going to bed late, like a little kid staying up past their bedtime. It was cute, when it didn't keep me awake. Anyway, I knew she'd be up, if I could find her apartment. I couldn't remember the number, and it wasn't posted on the floor call buttons, like it is in most apartment buildings. I decided to try asking the person I'd followed in, since they'd not yet made it to their room, but he didn't know of any Emmas. Well, it was a big building.

I tried the third floor. I knew her room number started with a three. From there, I think it ended with a 2, or maybe it was a letter. Fuck, I don't remember anything, and none of this looks familiar. I heard high-pitched laughter coming from one of the rooms, and I considered knocking on the owner's door. Hesitated. It was almost ten, is it rude to bother people that late? Then I sucked it up and knocked.

She was in a black polyester robe when she answered the door. It was tied in the front, a loose knot that allowed the front to open a little. Raven hair darker than the robe draped over her chest, so I wasn't able to get a good look at anything. A brief glimpse inside and I saw another girl, cross-legged on the linoleum. She puts her hand up in greeting, and I give a quick wave back.

 "Hey," I stuttered, caught off-guard by the greeter's face. It's perfect. A sharp jawline leading into a smooth chin. Her nose isn't so sharp, though, almost a button. I wanted to ask if she's Russian, but I knew that'd sound stupider than just the "hey."
 "Hey," she said, giving a movie star-quality chuckle.
 "What do you want?" the girl on the floor asked, her voice cacophonic in the nearly-naked room. The T.V.'s on. VH1.

I'm not normally at a loss for words, but here I felt awkward, barging in on them like this.

 "Emma," I said, "does she live on this floor?"
 "Sure, she used to," the raven-haired girl in front of me said. Holy shit, I loved her voice. It was soft but forceful. She didn't feel threatened by a random guy coming to her room in the middle of the night.

"Oh, she doesn't anymore?"

"No, she moved out about a month ago," she said. I think she's a little tentative. "Why'd you want that bitch anyway?"

"We used to fuck," I said. Something told me bluntness would go a long way with her.

She smirked. "You're a horn dog."

"Nah, I'm a guy." I smirked back. I thought, *she likes me.*

"Fair enough." She had been standing between me and the room, but then she stepped over to hold the door. "You wanna join us for a little bit?"

Yeah, she liked me. "Abso-fucking-lutely."

I didn't fuck her that night. We just sat and watched VH1. I don't even remember the show, just something shitty. We talked a lot, about where we worked, what we did. Marla was the gorgeous girl who greeted me, and Tina was the one who preferred the floor to the couch. Marla worked in a coffee shop – I could've guessed, her combat boots were too alternative to work anywhere else – and Tina was finishing a degree. I couldn't remember if she said Bachelor's or Master's, but it didn't really matter anyway. She was fuckable, but not who I would've picked between the two of them, so why should I have cared?

I learned from the two of them that Emma had moved back with her parents. She was failing out of school, or some shit like that. It was unfortunate, but it was actually kind of serendipitous for me, since I got to meet Marla. Emma moving out was apparently a second Christmas for both Marla and Tina. They didn't say what happened, but it didn't seem to be good. I wanted to ask, but they changed the subject, and I guess I forgot.

I stayed past two in the morning before I decided to leave – they probably would've let me crash on the couch if I'd wanted – and I woke up late the next day. Fortunately, I had evening shifts at the restaurant, so I wasn't missing much of anything.

When I got there, we were swamped, but again, there was no way I was going to focus on that job. But fuck Emma, this time I wanted to text

Marla – too bad she didn't give me her number. I decided to go back after the shift, just to grab the number and go.

Ugh, but that would've been too desperate. I still just wanted to get laid, and I wasn't sure if Marla would be into fucking. Too bad Emma had moved away – she was always into me, even after I broke it off.

I got a text from a number not registered in my phone.
"Daniel?" it said.

It was hard to wait a couple minutes before replying. I took two tables' orders out to keep my boss happy, but also to make those seconds go faster. The customers knew my laughs were manufactured, but I didn't care – she'd somehow gotten my number.

"Is this Marla?" I sent back when I returned to the kitchen.
"Tina." The text back was immediate, and I could feel my face droop. Shit. This isn't what I wanted.
"Oh, hey," I say. It was only through text, but I'm sure she knew how disappointed I was.
"I found your number on Facebook," she says. I didn't know what to reply, so I just let it go. A few minutes after: "It was for Marla, if that matters."
I still didn't really know how to answer, so I quickly sent, "Yeah?" and turned back to work.
"Wanna come over tonight?"
Holy fuck. Yes. Fuck yes I want to come over tonight.
It was hard to wait again – I really wanted them to know I had things going on, even though I was excited to see them. To see Marla.
I worked harder than I'd ever worked at that stupid restaurant, but the preoccupation didn't make time move any faster.

I knocked on the door, and I heard from the inside, "Come in!" Tina. Damn it, if Marla was so into me, why was Tina the one talking to me?

The scene when I walked in was almost identical to the last time. On one end of the room, a relatively small flat screen sat on an equally small table, with Tina plopped a few feet in front of it, cross-legged. On the opposite wall of the small living room, Marla sprawled on the two-person couch. She was in a skirt, and I pretended not to notice her splayed legs. I wished she wasn't wearing underwear. I also wished I'd be able to take them off for her.

I stood, staring at the TV without saying anything – VH1 again – and Marla sat up, patting the seat next to her. "Are you really not gonna sit down?"

I didn't say anything, but I eagerly sat next to her.
Tina turned around and gave me a shy half smile, which I did my best to return.

Marla reached next to her and put something in her mouth. I stared, and watched her do it again. They're colorful, but I couldn't tell what they were.

She saw me staring. "Want some?"
"I can't even tell what they are," I laughed.
"Gummy bears, stupid," she threw some at me. As a mock show of dominance, I ate the ones that landed on me.

She chucked a few more then stood up, putting her hand on my leg to push herself up. I wished she'd have left it there longer, or moved it up my leg, or something.

Leaning down next to Tina, she said something I didn't hear, then they both looked at me before making a show of going to the bathroom together. I continued to eat the gummy bears on my lap – I knew girls often partnered up for trips like that.

When they came out, they were giggling about something, but honestly, I didn't really care what. Marla hopped on the couch next to me, but about as far away as she could be on the couch. I guessed the leg-touching thing had passed. Tina went into her bedroom and a few seconds later came back with a large fleece blanket.

"Scooch," she commanded.

"Where?" I said. "This couch is only so big, y'know."

That was when I felt Marla's slender hands grip my shoulders and yank me toward her. I had to pretend like I was protesting a little bit, but at that point, I loved the contact. She let me nearly fall into her lap. I grazed her tits on the way down.

Tina turned off the lights before squishing next to me, and me, being between both her and Marla, let my thighs come in contact with each of theirs. We worked the blanket over us, but I doubt any of us were cold, being that close to each other. I felt a little cramped, but I didn't know if they were just into this kind of thing, so I didn't put my arms out.

Then Tina pulled her legs up, leaning onto me a little, and I saw in the flickering light of the TV, her arm reaching over my leg. I think I gulped pretty hard, but I didn't stop her. Then, she cupped my crotch, and I'm certain she could feel me get hard.

"So," Marla said, completely oblivious to Tina fondling me, "do you still talk to Emma? Like, ever?"

"Fuck, no," I say, and I know at that point my voice broke a little.

"Good," Marla said, then leaned into me, putting her hand on my thigh. I made eye contact with her – they were emerald – and leaned in to kiss her. I could feel Tina undoing my belt, and I hoped I knew where this was going.

Marla let me kiss her, and she moved her hand up my thigh. In just a few seconds, I had two girls' hands stroking my cock, and I was doing my best not to laugh – this was fucking great.

Marla stopped kissing me and kissed a line to my ear. Her voice was breathy, high, not the normal alto she possessed. "Bedroom?"

Oh, fuck yes. "Now," I said.

Tina and Marla each took one of my hands and led me into Tina's bedroom, shut the door. Tina tore her shirt off almost as soon as she shut the door. Even with her bra on, I could tell she had good tits. I hoped Marla's were better.

Marla, however, was pulling my pants off around my ankles, while I took off my shirt. Tina was waiting on her bed, naked, before Marla had lost any clothing.

"You gonna join us?" I teased, reaching for the bottom of her shirt.
She smirked, pulled my hand off. "Let me do that for you."
I watched her do it slowly – like she'd practiced – and I loved it. A personal striptease from Marla, with her sexy roommate just behind me. Marla stepped toward the bed with her underwear still on, and I pulled her to my chest. "You need to lose the bra," I said, undoing it for her. She let me, and when she pulled back to let it fall off, I almost gasped. Flawless.

"Shit you have good tits."
She laughed. "Thanks, you have a good cock." As if to prove her point, she started stroking it, but Tina gently pushed her off.
"That's mine," she said.

Marla shrugged and leaned for my face, started making out with me. I felt Tina slide onto my cock – damn, she was tight. Obviously no virgin, but pretty close. I fondled Marla's tits until she swung a leg over me, straddled my chest. "Mind if I sit on your face?"
I was internally begging her to.
"Go for it." Had to be cool, obviously.
She rode my face, and I grabbed every part of her ass that I could – it was so soft, smooth and full. Damn, she had a good body.
I was close and must've groaned or something, because I heard Tina say, "Not inside me!" Guess she wasn't on the pill.
She hopped off, and Marla went down with her. She'd finished a few minutes prior, but she told me to keep going anyway.

They kissed (hot), and Marla started sucking my cock. After a few seconds, I started to cum, and she pulled off. They both took my load on their faces. That was my second threesome, and man, was it perfect.

A few days later, Marla and I became fuck buddies, and we hooked up probably five times a week, even though I lived in uptown and she was downtown. I wanted her, and I used pretty much any means necessary to have her.

Things got a little awkward after the threesome, though.
"Hey, why does Tina always stay in her room when I'm over?"
"I don't know," Marla said, shrugging. "I think she was into you, maybe."
"Oh," I said. It was sort of obvious in retrospect, since she was the one who initiated everything with the threesome. And she definitely giggled about it more than Marla. Maybe she thought that Marla would be her way to get to me. Guess that backfired.

"Yeah," Marla said. "Plus, she's got school all the time at this point."
"NYU?" I asked, but I didn't care.
Marla nods. "Yeah, majoring in Interior Design. Gonna be rich."
"Nice." I wouldn't mind being rich, but I still liked Marla more. She was alternative – weird hairstyle, dyed, baggy, old clothing –but without the pretentiousness and condescension. Would've asked her out if I'd thought she would be into that. Probably the "I don't need a relationship to say I'm in love" kind of feminist. Didn't really matter that much anyway, as long as we were fucking as much as we were.

"Hey, what are we?" Marla asked one day during sex.
My hands were clamped around her perfect ass, pulling her into me. But I stopped when she asked that. "What do you want us to be?"
"I dunno," she said. Then, "Sorry, keep going."
I finished after an uncomfortable few minutes, neither of us closing our eyes or really enjoying it. Well, I enjoyed it a little, but her question made it weird.
"Do you like me?" she asked.
"Well, obviously," I said. "Why else put my cock in you all the time?"

She didn't appreciate my joke. "No, I mean, do you love me?"
Shit, I don't know. Probably not.
"I don't think so," I said, but I knew that wasn't good enough. "I like you a lot. You're sexy, and when we fuck, it's so great."
"You just like my body," she said. It hurt when she said it – it was completely void of any emotion.

And I wasn't really able to challenge her. Any time I went over, it was to fuck. We never went on dates or just hung out. I mean, sometimes we watched TV, but that was just when it was 2 am and Tina had exams the next day.

That was it. I spent the night, falling asleep instantly, but the next day I had images of Marla tossing next to me, unable to be comfortable next to me anymore.

I had gotten used to feeling awkward around Tina because of how she acted, but with Marla, it was different. It felt like I hurt her, just because I couldn't force feelings about her. I was honest, and it still wound up in making her distant. So once I left the next morning, I never went back. Neither of them texted me, either. I imagine Marla and I would be okay if we were to talk now, but I'd rather not risk any more bitterness with her. And besides, I like who she was, not whomever she may be now.

The Girl in the Yellow Shirt

Days went forward. I knew I was a little egotistical with the way I carried myself after Marla and Tina, however I didn't try to appear with such an ego with friends. Still working at the restaurant, I decided to head to that God-forsaken mall that I have been so accustomed too. I looked around for some shirts, and maybe a book or two if something caught my eye. It was bright as day, listening to music in my car and sipping on some coffee early that morning. The parking lot was empty and I had parked my car next to an old white sedan. I hopped out of my car pulled my shirt down a little bit, and heard crying that sounded muffled. I looked around and saw a girl crying in her car diagonally parked from me.

"Okay… weird." I told myself.

She was hunched in her driver's seat leaning on the window sobbing. Knees were brought to her chest. Her hands would brush through her hair and wipe the tears away from her eyes. I started to continue walking past the vehicle and stopped. I looked around once more, thinking if something bad happened around here. I took a deep breath and turned around walking towards her car. I tapped on the window.

"Hey..uh – you alright?" I asked.

She continued crying, as if I didn't exist. I tapped on the window again.

"Hey…" I said and stood there for a second. She didn't even look at me.
"Well, okay, just trying to help," I said and walked towards the mall.

I couldn't find any shirts that I liked and the books that were being advertised weren't to my liking. I browsed the bookstore for a few hours and decided that I should probably look at some shorts while I was there. I had been at the mall for almost three hours. As soon as I walked back out to my vehicle the girl in the yellow shirt was still crying, except this time she wasn't screeching through her car.

I unlocked my car and jumped in, ignoring her completely. As soon as I started to back out of the parking space I heard a horn. I looked in my rearview mirror and saw nobody driving behind me. I looked at the sedan where the girl had been crying she was looking right at me. I could've drove off. But something felt like I shouldn't.

I put my car back into drive and parked back. Turning off the engine I looked at her briefly for a second and she seemed to make an attempt to smile. I sighed and hopped out of the car and leaned on my hood.

Her window rolled down, I squinted my eyes and tilted my head.

"Hey, I'm sorry about earlier." She says sniffling.

"Is everything okay?" I asked. "You've been here for a while." I said.

"Not really." She says to me.

I sighed again and walked toward her window. "Why are you crying here by yourself?"

"It's a long story," She tells me.

I remember Thomas and Tyler, and how they would take time to listen to me. I figure it wouldn't hurt to see if she could spill the beans in regards to what was causing her so much emotional stress.

"Sometimes strangers can be the best listeners." I tell her.
She laughs and rolls her eyes. "Yeah okay." She says.
"Well alright." I say turning around. "Hope things get better." I say unlocking my car.

As soon as I open the door she sticks her head out of the window.

"Wait!" I hear her say. I close my car door and for a second look onto the traffic in front of me than at her.

"What?" I say.

"You have a minute?" She asks.

"Sure." I said leaning on the hood of my car.

"You can sit in here if you want." She tells me.

I walk over to her passenger side door and open it hoping that she wasn't going to shoot me or try something odd. She looked young, most likely still in high school and having issues with friends.

"What's the issue?" I asked looking outside of her window.

She laughed for a brief second and then placed her hands on her temples.

"Uhm." She finally smiled. "This is so weird to me." She says.

"Well sitting in a parking lot for a few hours crying is weird to me." I tell her.

"Fair." She says.

"All of my friends are no longer my friends." She utters.

"Why are they no longer your friends?" I ask.

"They found out I slept with my now, ex-boyfriend."

She started to twiddle her thumbs going back and forth between that and biting at her fingernails.

"There has got to be more than that." I tell her starting to laugh. "I mean c'mon was he someone else's boyfriend?"

"No." She said looking down on her lap.

"Okay what is it then?" I asked. "There's more- spill it." I add.

"I go to a private Christian school." She tells me.

"That just made a lot more sense." I tell her. "So now they all think you're this terrible person for having sex?" I asked.

"I am." She said as tears began to pour out of her eyes.

"I don't think you're a terrible person." I tell her.

I watched as tears dropped on her lap. She leaned her head on the window again looking onto the empty side of the parking lot. It took her a second to calm down.

"I was going to wait until I was married." She tells me. Her voice started to cut off as she began crying again. "I thought I was going to be with him for the rest of my life." She says.

I wanted to slap her and tell her things would be fine and it wasn't the end of the world. She became so hysterical to the point where I almost grabbed her phone and called her parents.

"And you know what the stupidest thing is?" She said angrily.
"What is that?" I ask.
"All his friends are okay with the fact we had sex." She says pounding on her steering wheel. "They think I'm just some whore." She adds.
She started to cry more as I sat there awkwardly looking outside of her car window. She started to catch her breath and began to control her breathing.
"I don't want to go to school today." She tells me pressing her lips together.
"I wanted to kill myself." She added.
"Yeah I wanted to at one point as well." I told her.
"Why?" She asked.
I looked at her and lifted an eyebrow. My lips shifted the right and my eyes focused outside of her window then at her.
"You tell me your reasons first." I say.
"I told you why." She says to me.
"You told me why you're crying. Not why you wanted to kill yourself." I said to her.
She was quiet for a few seconds, I could hear her exhale and the skin rubbing of her twiddling thumbs. She looked at me.

"I feel trapped." She says staring at me. "I feel like I don't have a mother or a father." She added.

"I put everything into my ex-boyfriend, and when we broke up…." She stopped and shrugged her arms.

"You felt you had nobody there for you?" I asked.

"None of my friends talked to me." She said smirking. "And I can't talk to my parents about it."

"Because they would be disappointed?" I asked.

"I wouldn't want to know what they would do." She tells me. "Probably send me off to an all-girls school." She noted.

"When were you trying hurt yourself?" I asked her.

"Today." She said with her eyes beginning to water. "I wanted to take this car and just stop everything," She tells me.

I stayed quiet and thought about her situation for a minute.

"How about you?" She said crossing her arms.

"We're on the same boat." I tell her smiling.

"What do you mean?" She asked.

"I dated a girl for a while, broke up, and I don't really talk to my mother or father." I tell her.

"I was probably your age." I say to her.

"How old are you now?" She asked.

"I'm 19 now, almost 20." I say to her. "This was 4 years ago." I add.

"And you decided not to?" She asked me.

"Oh no, I tried." I told her. "Tried to hang myself in a closet." I added.

"Well you're still here." She said.

"I broke my closet shelves." I told her. "I passed out but it was a poor attempt," I tell her laughing.

"You didn't try again?" She asked me.

"There's more to look forward to." I told her. "There's always more." I say.

I spent about a good hour or two talking to her. Her phone was buzzing off of people trying to get ahold of her. She never answered it, I found she played the violin and that she also ran track in school. She started to appear better and I had mentioned to her that I should be on my way.

"You'll be alright." I told her. "Things get better." I said.
"I hope so." She said as I closed her door and smiled at her. I took a deep breath and sighed as I got into my car. I watched her drive off past me hoping that she wouldn't do anything stupid.
While I was driving I thought to myself. "What the fuck was her name?"

I went home and opened up a brown journal I kept hidden in the air vent of my room. Somewhere my parents wouldn't look. I noted everything that she had mentioned to me that day. I also took the time to review all the girls, other than the ones that I have dated in my journal. I remembered how hurt she was and I hoped I wasn't the guy who did that to one of the names that I leered at in my journal.

There were so many women that I had left out as well. One's whom I thought were just a 'fling' and that there was no relationship to develop. I sat in silence in my room crying and re-reading everything I wrote about some of the girls. Rachelle? Oh yes I remember her, she was at that party where she almost tore my dick off she was so bad at hand jobs. Jade? Ah yes, She couldn't even kiss me without her teeth getting in the way. I started to look at all the little things of various women that I didn't even give a shot at for a relationship. The smallest things. I figured if I had continued doing so I would end up alone.

I started to think that maybe my parents were just trying their ways of parenting. They aren't perfect, hell; nobody is--not myself for certain.

As soon as my dad had left for work one morning I planned to talk to my mom, and see if she would be able to understand what I have been going through for the past few years. Private moments I kept to myself, thoughts that were only whispered under my breath in my darkest moments. I hoped that my mother would understand and display a sense of care that I have long yearned for. I couldn't even remember if my father and I have even played catch together. The reason being is because he and I never spent any quality time together doing anything. I remembered everything from my childhood. I remembered my youngest days. Because even then I was alone to play with toys and not focused on hand in hand with my parents… Things had to change, and I had to make them change for the better.

I didn't sleep on my bed that night. I wondered about the girl in the yellow shirt. I placed my brown journal back in the vent and slept next to the cold air blowing in my face.

Valerie

A year and a half went by and there were no women in my life other than my mother. Sooner or later, some friends who at one point appeared devoted, disappeared. Tracy split herself away from Luke and I, Tyler joined the military service, and I was still working my job at the restaurant. Being chaste for a year felt refreshing. There were many other things that I decided to change.

One evening, Luke invited me out to the bar, so I gave Thomas a call as well. We were near the local university and planned for a good night out with only us three.

"Let's go check out the gay bar," Thomas said jokingly.
"Alright, I'm down, let's go," Luke said, beginning to laugh.
As soon as we walked by the bar, Luke opened the door and went in.
"I'm not going in there, dude," I told him.
"I haven't actually been here, let's see what's inside," he told Thomas and I.

I slapped my forehead and began rubbing my eyes. Fucking Luke was putting us in a very uncomfortable spot. But why not? Let's go and check out a gay bar for once. As soon as we walked in, we were immersed in flashing lights and guys dressed as drag queens. Luke sat down on a barstool and Thomas and I followed, sitting next to him.

"This is hilarious," Luke said, starting to laugh uncontrollably.
"Yeah, there are guys here looking at us weird," Thomas replied.
"Relax, let's just get a drink and we'll go to a different bar," Luke told us.

I remember I asked for a shot of whiskey and when the bartender poured my drink, he winked at me.

"Yep, that's it, we're getting out of here, dude," I told Thomas and Luke.
"Alright, let's go out the back," Luke said.

We stopped in the smoking section by the back entrance to choose where to go next. We pulled out cigarettes and scrolled through our options on our phones.

"Excuse me," a voice said behind me.
"What's up?" I look away from my phone at a girl. She was holding a beer, an unlit cigarette in her mouth.
"Do you gentlemen have a lighter?" she asked.
"Only if you smoke it here with us," Luke said to her.
She had dark hair and brown eyes. Her glasses made her look like a cute librarian, at least I thought so.
"Sure," she said, grabbing the lighter from Luke and lighting her cigarette. "So, what are you boys doing here?" she asked, handing the lighter back.
I laughed and looked at Luke. "We're here for our friend," I told her.
"Are you guy's gay?" she asked us.
All three of us started to shake our heads 'no.' As soon as she popped the question, Thomas started coughing from his cigarette.
"Then why are you here?" she asked.
"Well Luke is, we're here for him," Thomas said, laughing.
"Fuck you guys," Luke said, putting his cigarette out.
"What's your name?" I asked her.
"Valerie," she answered and held out her hand.

We talked to her while we finished our cigarettes and when we left, we invited her to bring her friends and come with us. Thomas didn't seem comfortable of the idea but he got over it without complaint.

She had three friends with her, two of them guys and, as you could probably guess, they were gay. The last was a girlfriend that she said was bisexual.

Later that evening, drinks were drunk and urinated. Time flew by and the bars were announcing last calls. I got Valerie's number and thought about sending her a text in a couple days.

Within a few weeks of hanging out with each other, we were dating. Our relationship wasn't 'official,' just dinner dates, movie nights and hanging out with friends. My emotions weren't confusing and she seemed pretty straightforward. I assumed she was bisexual like her girlfriend, but never wanted to ask.

One evening, she invited me over her apartment for dinner and a movie. She cooked like a professional. I remember those tacos being exquisite.

I started to do the dishes for her, wiping off a plate I had in my hand, and taking hers as she finished up.

"Hey, you want me to throw these in the dishwasher?" I asked, opening it as I spoke.
"Yeah, that's fine," she told me.

There were a brief five seconds after she said 'that's fine,' before she jumped and screeched, "OH NO DON'T OPEN THE DISHWASHER!" But she was too late and what I found turned my face red.

I recovered and started to laugh, pulling out a black butt plug.

"Dude, no way," I said, waving it at her.

She began to smile and grabbed for it. "It's not mine," she said, her face turning red.

"It's the dishwasher's right?" I asked, laughing.

"Shut up!" she said, grabbing it out of my hand.

That was the end of it then, but we talked about it with time, even so, she wasn't completely open with me. All the time we had spent together was driving me crazy. Being with her made her more desirable, it created a sexual tension.

A month flew by, there was a lot of kissing and touching. No sex. At the time I was OK with that. But she popped the question over a night out drinking. We had met up at the same bar and talked about our days, just us, no friend at all.

"Why... haven't we had sex?" she asked, stabbing the ice with her straw.

"I don't know how to answer that," I told her. Of course, asking her to have sex with me now would turn me off and probably her as well.

"We don't really need to rush anything," I told her, smiling and sipping on my drink.

Valerie stopped stabbing her ice. She pressed her lips together and she slowly tilted her head.

"Huh..." she said, tilting her head, "That's different."

"How is that different?" I asked her, "I'm sure there are plenty of guys who would do the same."

"I'm sure there are." she said. "I really like foreplay though and getting oral sex."

"Duly noted," I said to her.

We laughed and stopped talking about it. We met up with some friends and finished the night at the bar.

We made plans the next weekend to go to a wedding dinner. The week before the dinner, we saw each other daily. I slept over some nights, and on one of those, along with all the kissing and touching, I decided to take a little risk. Valerie sat on her bed that night reading for school with those sexy glasses.

"Whatever happened to that black butt plug?" I asked her, giggling.
"In my drawer," she told me, "Why?"
"Curious," I said, smiling. A black dress on a hanger was hanging off the doorknob of her closet. "Is this what you're wearing to dinner?" I asked, gesturing at it.
"Yes, what does this have to do with the butt plug?" she asked back.
I walked over to her drawer and pulled it out, there was a wireless remote with it. I walked back over to her dress.
"Colors match," I told her.
Valerie froze for a second. I saw her half-ass smirk before she hid it with her book.
"What are you saying?" she asked, placing the book on her stomach, smiling.
"I'm saying, since you own this... you're obviously into it," I told her.
"Obviously," she replied.
I sat on the bed next to her, she knew where this was going.
"Can we make this dinner interesting?" I asked her.
She stared at me, her cheeks red and eyes wide open.
"You're serious?" she asked, sitting up.
I couldn't tell which way she was leaning. So I played stupid and shrugged my shoulders. "Ok, never mind," I told her, putting the plug back into her drawer.
I started to watch T.V until she put her book down again.

"I'll think about it," she said.

"OK," I replied, acting as if her final decision didn't matter. But don't get me wrong, I would have loved for her to say yes.

"What do I get out of it?" she asked me.

"Whatever you want," I told her, shrugging my shoulders and looking at the T.V.

One day and then a second went by. Valerie did not bring up my idea. But as soon as I got to her apartment the night of the dinner, she disappeared into the bathroom. As soon as she walked out she grabbed my arm and kissed me.

"Thirty minutes and I'm taking it out," she told me.

"What are you talking about?" I asked her.

"It's already there," she said, looking at me.

My eyes widened and my mouth opened as I processed exactly what she was telling me.

"Where's the remote?" I asked her.

"Why do we need that?" she asked.

"See I don't know if you're lying to me right now," I told her.

Valerie grabbed my hand and led it up her skirt, I could feel the end of it right where it should be. She let go of my hand and shoved a Ziplock into her purse.

"Don't turn it up all the way or it'll make noise," she said, handing me the remote.

'Whoa, no way,' I thought to myself.

"You're driving. Let's go," she said, turning off the lights to her apartment.

I watched how she walked in heels so she wouldn't fall over. I had a thought of turning it on at the highest speed as she walked down the few steps. But, of course, I wouldn't do that.

We got into my car and I instantly pulled out the remote.

"This is so cool," I said looking at it, "How do you turn it on?"

"It's already on," she said.

"Oh," I moved a knob on the remote.

"Ffffuck..." Valerie uttered and began to claw at my passenger door handle.

My eyes widened and I looked at her. I turned the knob off for a second, smiled, and turned it back on. Off, and then on. Off… and on I felt like a kid on Christmas who just got his first Lego set with a crane and construction equipment.

"OK, OK," she said.

"Alright," I told her, leaving it off and smiling.

"30 minutes," she said as we begin to drive off.

We got to the resort and walked over to the restaurant where everyone was waiting.

She grabbed onto my arm and whispered to me, "Can you tell... from behind."

"Nope, already checked," I told her.

We sat down at a long table and greeted her friends. Knowing what I did, watching her hug the bride to be and being introduced around was comical. As soon as we ordered food I felt the inside pocket of my blazer to ensure I could locate the knob.

I wasn't mean. I waited until she was done with her food and conversation was whirling around the table before I moved the knob to 'ON.'

She was talking to a girl across the table from us. The girl was blonde, with curly hair and I did what any guest would do. I listened...

"It all depends on my GPA this semester," Valerie was saying to her. As soon as I turned on the device, her hand grabbed my knee and shook.

"You'll be fine," I said to her, "What is your GPA at now?"
As soon as she began to talk I turned the knob a little more.
"It's uhm-it's good enough right now," She told me, squeezing my knee a little more.

I could see the facial expressions she was trying to hide while her friend was speaking to her. Honestly, I was getting turned on myself watching her fight it. It had also been way passed thirty minutes and I was surprised that she hadn't gone to the restroom yet and put it in that Ziploc bag.

She grabbed her phone while her friend talked to her.
"I'm listening, just checking e-mail," she told her.
I looked at my phone and saw a text message.
"dick," it read.

I casually reached in my blazer, as if I had an itch. I turned the knob, just smidge. Valerie sat straight up and began to drink water. By then, I was incredibly turned on. I had to position myself differently to accommodate.

"Are you two staying around the resort for tonight?" the blonde headed girl asked us.
As soon as Val was about to speak, I stepped in. "I'd like to," I told her.
"Up to her though," I added, smiling at Valerie. "I mean, I wouldn't

mind drinking tonight," I said to the blonde girl, I held out my hand, "What's your name again?"

"Rebecca," she said, smiling and shaking my hand across the table.

"The room is on me," I told Valerie and squeeze her knee.

Valerie took a deep breath and let out. "We can do that," she said, grabbing my groin from under the table. "I do want to get a drink though," Valerie said, looking at Rebecca.

"No-no let me get it," I said, getting up, "Stay here, what do you want?"

I didn't know if she was going to go to the bathroom to take it out while I was gone. But I could tell she was having fun with me being somewhat of an ass.

I walked over to the bar and waited for the bartender. While he was making drinks, I thought to myself, '*I wonder how far this thing reaches*?' All the drunkards at the bar wouldn't notice. I reached into my blazer and turned the knob all the way up then quickly off. I turned around and looked at Valerie, smiling. She had just put her phone down. I waited to see a message on mine.

"Seriously!"

I brought our drinks to the table, and turned the knob back on while placing my wallet in the same pocket.

"We should get that room before they're all booked," Valerie said, grabbing my groin again.

"You guys want to come to the pool later?" Rebecca asked us.

Valerie had found my erection in my slacks. She started to rub her hand on my cock.

I didn't know what to do, I couldn't stand up. I reached in my blazer once more and turned the knob at least halfway. Valerie stopped and looked at me.

"It's up to the boss," I said, looking at Valerie.

"Of course, is your hubby coming?" Valerie asked. Her eyes closed for a second and opened. It was noticeable, at least, to me.

"Yeah, we were already planning on it," Rebecca said to us.

"I'm going to get the room then," I said to Valerie.

As I began to walk towards the reservation desk, I turned the device off and came back with our room keys.

Valerie smiled at me as I returned, "I didn't bring any extra clothes," she told Rebecca, "Or a swimsuit."

"Yeah me neither," I mentioned.

"I got you," Rebecca said to Valerie.

"I'll go swimming in my underwear," I said, laughing, "I really don't care."

"Men have it easy," Rebecca said to me.

"You ready?" Valerie said, standing up. "We're going to stop in our room real quick," she said to Rebecca.

"Have fun," she said, smiling.

"Oh, we will be right back," Valerie told her.

"Oh, please, take your time," Rebecca said to her.

Valerie and I started to walk back to our room. The property was beautiful and the few people walking around with a drinks in their hands were friendly. As soon as we got into a hallway where our room was, I pulled out the card key.

Valerie stopped me and stared. She pushed me up against our hotel room door and began kissing me.

"Turn it on..." she said, kissing my neck.

I reached in my blazer and switched it on.

"Higher..." she said.

I moved the knob once and began to kiss her lips.

She stopped and placed her head on my shoulders. "Oh…fffuck…" murmured out of her mouth. "All the way," she said, reaching down into my slacks. I turned the knob as far as I could.

"Ohh ssshit," she uttered.

I placed the key card in the door and grabbed her by the hand. We walked into the room and she leaned against the wall.

I looked at her for a second then walked towards her. I lifted up her dress and started kissing her neck. She had one of her hands on my back, with the other, she grabbed my belt and removed it. Both her hands grabbed my waist. She moved down with my slacks.

"No," I told her, "You've done enough for me."
She stood back up and looked at me, "What do you mean?"

I smiled and picked her up, wrapping her legs around my waist. I threw her on the bed and wrapped one arm under her leg. I put the other on her hip and dragged her toward the edge of the bed. I kissed her ear, sucked on her neck and moved down towards her waist. Tasting her, I could hear that butt plug vibrating. I placed two fingers inside her and allowed her to enjoy herself.

"Get inside me already," she said, pulling at my hair.
I pushed inside.
"Holy shit," came tumbling out of my mouth.
Her legs went around my hips. I could feel her tongue running up and down my neck. I didn't even find it creepy.
She grabbed my fingers and began sucking on them. Then she pushed me off and turned around, putting her head on the pillow and her ass

up. I pushed inside her again and put my hand on the plug that had been vibrating inside her.

"FUCK," she said loudly.

My hands ran up her back to her hair. I grabbed it and pulled her up until her face was next to mine and her back was arched. I reached around her, grabbing her breast and sucking on her neck.

There was a point where I didn't know how fast we were fucking each other. She was moaning uncontrollably, and I couldn't help to do the same. All that sexual tension that had been building up was being released. It felt amazing.

I pulled out and came on the bed. I was entirely out of breath and didn't want to move. I reached over to the side of the bed and turned the knob off. I could hear her catching her breath as I caught mine.

"Oh fuck," she said, letting out air.
"Fuck," I said, turning my head to her.

We laid on the bed for a good minute or two before she got up, using the wall to keep her balance on her way to the bathroom. She came back around the corner back to bed and plopped down.
I started laughing. She crawled towards me and lifted up my arm, wrapping it around herself.

"We still need to go to the pool," she said to me.
"Ok, let's do it," I told her, laughing.

As time continued, we separated. She went to medical school. I remember her coming to my house to talk about it. I was sad to see her go, tears came to my eyes and I tried to act like 'more of a man' by holding them back. With her car packed and a glimmer on her face I wondered if we were ever 'together.'

It was one of the best times I had… I don't know if I should've said I loved her. But that word had hurt me in the past. Valerie was gone I was happy for her and happy for where she decided to go in life. She had taken her time to know me for my substance. She had listened to everything I had to say. Sex had been the last thing her and I focused on. I looked back at the time her and I had together and remembered how she had treated me. She had cooked for me, I'd cooked for her. We had laughed about stupid things. Enjoyed each other's company and spent time together. It genuinely felt that she had liked me for my volume as a person. As soon as she left I missed her and only had memories.

"I will see you again," she told me.

I watched her get into her car. I closed her door with my heart in my throat. I sat by the front gate of my parents' house as she drove out of my neighborhood. Out of my arms and, what it felt like, out of my life.

🐇 <u>Whitney</u> 🐇

With all my past love experiences, my most recent being Valerie, I felt that I knew what I was looking for in a companion. I was chaste for another year and a half before I met Whitney. There isn't much detail I'd like to mention. We got married in April. I signed a contract with the military and we took our marriage from there. With everything I had been through, I figured that I could handle a marriage. Always being committed to the one I desired most.

Within time, Whitney and I divorced. I found numerous messages in her phone from an ex-boyfriend, she'd violated her vows. She packed her things and left while I was on a training exercise.

She tried to collect money and demanded items that she left behind. It was some of the worst pain I had ever felt. She took the dog I had gotten for our family.

As soon as marriage had been brought into my life, I had placed effort into doing anything to fix it. However, more and more it seemed to me that I was someone who had to make someone happy without it being reciprocated. Lies, paranoia, the consistent nagging. No matter what I did right in my marriage I was still wrong.

When I look back at it now, I think to myself, 'Let her find happiness,' because there was a day when we were both happy. But some people don't know what a commitment is, they stay for a while and then they look for reasons not to be with you anymore. They'll search for your imperfections and not fix theirs. If you accept theirs, your kindness is taken for granted. Being too soft these days gets you nowhere.

When I came home to an empty apartment I felt remorseful and taken advantage of. I only wished that there had been more blissful days. However, like a child she had expected to be dazzled in sparkles, romanticized normally and expected flowers and presents all the time. She could never do anything like this for me. My efforts weren't appreciated, and my love wasn't enough. Her selfishness destroyed our marriage as I stood by helplessly. Arguments wouldn't fix anything and talking seemed to go nowhere.

In the end, everything made sense. Her father left her mother had refrained from further education just like her. And even though she deeply hurt me and I will never forgive her for the pain that she caused, I wish her the best. Our souls bonded and even though she is not here with me anymore, I throw out what caused me pain and remember what I learned.

Men should not need to be the enablers, the emotional support, money, you name it. As men, it is better for us to be chaste once in awhile, because there will be day when our emotions get the best of us. Throw away the thick skin and wait for Ms. Perfect to come. Without rushing anything, let her prove her worth to you. You do not need to prove yours by spending money, being poetic, or showing her you are a good listener. If a woman expects anything from you - Run... run as fast as you can. Leave and learn early. Expectations will only cause issues.

When it boils down to a lasting relationship, it requires respect for one another, kindness, and not having the fear of hurting one another's feelings. Without respect, the relationship will crumble; without kindness, nobody will talk; and if you are scared to hurt another's feelings, truth will not be told. Enduring a life of lustfulness will slow down the process and only delay what your heart *truly* desires.

I do believe there will be a day that I will find someone who can do so. Someone without a 'type' or a long line of 'expectations.' I look back at all the women I have been with and not furthered a relationship with, because I felt there was something missing. That they were not someone who talked to me, respected my substance as a person, and displayed enough caring that they could say something and hurt my feelings.

My heart has been pulled through enough, and it will take time to be ready again. I don't plan on re-marrying anytime soon. I sure don't go out looking to talk to women anymore. Still young, and with plenty of time to do these things later, I'll take more steps forward and explore the world for a while.

www.ingramcontent.com/pod-product-compliance
Lightning Source LLC
Chambersburg PA
CBHW031534040426
42445CB00010B/524